52
WEEKLY
Devotions
for
FAMILIES CALLED TO SERVE

Karen Whiting

 HENDRICKSON
PUBLISHERS

 ROSE KiDZ

52 Weekly Devotions for Families Called to Serve

RoseKidz® is an imprint of
Rose Publishing, LLC
P.O. Box 3473
Peabody, Massachusetts 01961-3473 USA
www.hendricksonrose.com/rosekidz

Interior design by Drew McCall
Cover design by Emily Heintz

Published in association with Books & Such Literary Management, 52 Mission Circle #122, PMB 170, Santa Rosa, CA 95409, www.booksandsuch.com.

ISBN: 978-1-62862-817-3
RoseKidz® Reorder #L50037
JUVENILE NONFICTION /Religious / Christian / Devotion & Prayer

Printed in the United States of America
Printed June 2019

Dedication

In appreciation for my family members who served:

- My grandfather John Hartigan who founded our town's fire department and served for four decades

- My father, John Hartigan Jr., who served in the U.S. Army in WWII

- My husband, Commander Jim Whiting, who served twenty-two years in the U.S. Coast Guard

- My son Michael Whiting who served in the U.S. Air Force

- My daughter Rebecca White who served as a disaster relief case manager for United Methodist Committee on Relief (UMCOR)

- My son-in-law Larry White who served in the U.S. Army

- My Uncle Dennis Hartigan who served in the U.S. Marine Corp during the Korean War

- My brother Jerome Hartigan who served in the U.S. Navy

- My brother-in-law Marty Maneker who served in the U.S. Army

- My brother-in-law Captain Bill Van Dyke who served in the U.S. Navy

- My brother-in-law Randy Pickering who served in the U.S. Army

- My uncle Bob Saars who served as a volunteer firefighter

- My cousin Sheila Basquil who serves as an emergency-room nurse

- My cousin Michael Doody who served as a police officer

- My father's cousins George and Ed Hartigan who served in the New York City Police Department

- For many others who volunteered and served in their churches and communities

Acknowledgments

Thanks to my agent, Rachel Kent, of Books and Such Literary Management and her great support as she comes alongside me in the publishing process.

Thanks to many families who provided stories for the book, including those who wish to remain anonymous. These are family members and workers on the frontlines serving people as first responders, military personnel, law enforcers, missionaries, and volunteers. They bless the people of this nation with their sacrifice and generosity.

I so appreciate the following people who shared their stories:

- Beth Brubaker
- Sheri Clark Burt
- Amy Rose Wells Fairchild, paramedic
- Karlie Harper
- Heidi Martin
- Jennifer Martinez
- Kristi Neace
- Tommy Neiman, firefighter, EMT
- Trevor Nelson, firefighter
- Ashley Stapleton
- Rebecca Love White, disaster relief case manager
- Peggy Sue Wells
- Bethany Yoder

Table of Contents

Dear Parents,

Every family is special. This book helps us understand the uniqueness of families who serve others in many different capacities. It will broaden your children's outlook and provide opportunities to discuss your own family's challenges.

I am the mother of five children. My late husband served in the United States Coast Guard. My father served in the Army Air Corps World War II (now the Air Force) and my mother was a nurse. In the town where I grew up, my grandfather served as fire chief of the volunteer fire department. With our children, we served our community when a major hurricane devastated the area, including our house. I understand the uniqueness of families who serve and the interruptions of family times due to emergencies and calls to serve. These are also opportunities to develop character in your children.

Our family often tailored devotions to fit our unique lifestyle. We wove faith into our daily family life and worked around a parent's schedule. We applied the scriptures through hands-on activities and chats that were relevant to our lives.

Family faith time doesn't have to be formal or rigid. Make it fun and do what works for your children and lifestyle. Some weeks you might fit in every activity and reading. That's great. Other weeks you might only have time to read the main scripture and story. That's wonderful, too. Cherish the moments you share faith. Create a faith scrapbook as you go through the book to capture the memories.

Be a family with the heart and commitment of Joshua 24:15 "As for me and my family, we will serve the LORD." Give your child the best possible gift to equip them for life.

Blessings,
Karen Whiting

Family Devotion Benefits and Tips

HOW: Start Simple

S Schedule time to gather together

I Involve your children

M Mix in fun and hands-on experiences

P Plan ahead and choose what you'll do before each week starts

L Let it become a legacy with capturing the memories

E End each one with prayer

Be Ready and Willing to Go the Distance

- Be committed
- Be consistent
- Be open-minded to children's responses and guide them to truth
- Be enthusiastic
- Be flexible
- Be realistic and understand your child's ability
- Be in the word yourself so you know the Bible

Benefits of Family Devotions

There are many spiritual and cognitive benefits of doing devotions. Here is a short list:

- Puts God first
- Provides a biblical world view for life
- Builds Bible literacy
- Maintains the role of parents as the spiritual leaders of their families
- Strengthens family bonds
- Focuses on God's perspective
- Helps families develop grateful hearts
- Promotes listening comprehension
- Builds reading comprehension
- Increases vocabulary
- Helps children learn to talk with adults

- Lays a foundation for talking as a family
- Helps children learn to apply what they learned
- Develops analytical skills and critical thinking
- Provides a way to transmit your core beliefs to your family
- It brings your family together on a regular basis

Family Devotions Your Way!

These are really do-votions. It's a combination of a devotion, hands-on activities, and topics to chat about. It gets you actively doing things as you study God's Word.

Your family can decide your level of commitment each week. Some weeks are harder than others and there's only time to read the devotion and maybe do a few chats in the car or put out supplies for family members to do an activity as they have time. Let it fit your lifestyle.

This book can help service families.

If your family includes a member who serves in the community or world, let this help you explore your unique lifestyle and trust God with your family's special concerns. Check the Frontline Tips for special ideas that help families who have the unique lifestyles of serving others, including in dangerous situations.

This book can help all families.

For any family, use this book to explore and understand people around you who serve in so many ways in the community, country, or world as military, first responders, missionaries, or volunteers in various churches and organizations. It's also an opportunity to pray for God's direction for each child's future. Consider as you read, how your family can volunteer or serve other people.

You choose your own way to do devotions!

Commit to one time a week as the launch day (that may actually vary) and one time to wrap it up. Let the rest be options to choose a la carte. Sometimes you can do it all, and some weeks may get so busy you can only do a little. Celebrate what you do get done.

Choose Your Family Style

Start the devotionals with the beginning of the year, the week you buy the book, the week a family member is deployed, or whatever time works best for your family.

- Start with an activity to introduce the concept and then read the devotions, or

- Start with the devotion, or

- Start with a scripture and Chat Prompts, and then add what looks doable that week.

For families with members who deploy or travel

- Buy two copies of this book—one copy for family at home and one book (or downloadable book) for the family member who is deployed

- Record sessions the traveling family member misses

- Do some Activity Options online

- Take lots of photos to bridge the distance for the member who is away

- Let the absent family member email about the week's topic

Each Devotion Week Includes:

- Scripture and focus for the week

- Three or four choices of activities

- One contemporary story to read and reflect on together

- Bible story to read and discuss

- Choices of Chat Prompts, usually paired with a Scripture, related to the theme

- Scrapbook/Prayer Journal Options to create a spiritual keepsake of your family's faith

- One or more Frontline Tips to provide tools to address unique challenges of families who serve

- Prayer for the week you can read once or say each day

- Wrap up to discuss the topic, activities, and what was learned

Activities and Chat Prompts

Don't feel like you need to do every activity every week. Choose what works. You can always go through the book again in a year or two and use different activities.

Note: For the Activity Options, check on age requirements and rules before offering to serve in your community.

Bible Story Connection

Part of doing devotions as a family is studying God's truth in the Bible. Make this exploration fun by engaging all the senses. Act out stories, retell them, and consider how to bring in aromas and sounds associated with each story.

Scrapbook/Prayer Journal Options

Transform the prompts into a keepsake that will help your family reflect and remember each week you did. You can buy a special book to journal in and add photos, or just staple sheets of paper together. Each week look for the suggestions of how to reflect and add memories to your scrapbook.

- Let children add dabs of watercolor, a drawing, or stamp design

- Write in words that became buzz words during the week

- Add fun stickers that relate to the week's theme

- Take photos of your family doing the activities and add them to the scrapbook

- Jazz it up as desired to express how your family responded to the topic

Prayer

Use the prayer throughout the week. Make copies and keep them handy for on-the-go moments. Keep track of prayer requests and answered prayers in your scrapbook/journal.

Wrap-Up

End each week with a brief time to chat about the topic and activities. Ask what each person learned and add those thoughts to the pages of your scrapbook/journal.

Start (or Restart) Any Week!

Don't wait for a new year to start family devotions. Start this week. Any time of year is a great time to start:

- Easter and new hope
- Spring and planting seed of faith
- Summer with a less rigid calendar
- Fall and the start of school
- Christmas or the New Year for new birth and new starts

1. As parents, read the opening and letter to parents.
2. If this is a restart, or you need motivation to persist, read the list of benefits and select the three top reasons you want to succeed at family devotions. Post those somewhere very visible for your family. Let those be your motivation or mottos to keep going.
3. Turn to the current week and get going!

Get Kids Excited About Devotions

1. **Talk the devotions up.**
Bring the devotion ideas into family meal times and drive times. Chat about the scriptures, talks, and activities.

2. **Capture the fun in pictures.**
Be sure to take photos of the activities when possible and build a family memory keepsake by adding the suggested art, thoughts, and photos to the scrapbook/prayer journal.

3. **Engage the senses.**
Use visuals and sounds affiliated with stories to deepen the impact. Act out passages. Why not cook foods that relate to Bible times? This helps children experience and understand Bible times.

4. **Pray with a prayer cup.**
Decorate a plastic cup with permanent makers. Cut slips of paper and write the names of each family member on one. At the end of each devotion, let each member draw a name to pray for that person. Or you can have someone draw one name at a meal and then, as a family, pray for that individual. If desired, add names of other family members and friends to pray for them.

5. Connect with one-on-one time.

Consider doing some activities with one child at a time. Children love this special bonding time with a parent.

6. Memorize the week's opening scripture.

Read the verse daily and talk about what it means. After a few days, say some of the words and see if they can finish the verse. Recite it together. Look up fun memory verse games online.

7. Provide each child with his or her own age-appropriate Bible.

Having their own Bibles helps increase their interest. You can also provide journals or prayer notebooks. Match these items to your children's ages and learning styles. Visual learners want more pictures and charts; analytical children enjoy charts and facts; social learners like profiles about people and places.

8. Share what you learn.

Invite friends to join you for some of the devotions. Share the memories and how the devotion time helps your family grow in faith and other areas.

Capturing Faith Memories

Family Beatitude: Happy is the family who captures memories, for they will build lasting bonds.

Focus: Building a legacy through captured memories

Weekly Bible Verse: *When the rainbow appears in the clouds, I will see it. I will remember that my covenant will last forever. It is a covenant between me and every kind of living creature on earth.* Genesis 9:16

Activity Options

☐ Start a family faith album to capture the memories of your faith journey. Use the ideas at the end of each unit to inspire you with what to draw or write. Snap photos and add those, too.

☐ God made a promise or special commitment with his people, called a covenant. He made one with Noah and Noah's family. Read about it in Genesis chapter nine. As a family make a commitment to God to follow him. Write it out and hang it up. Paint a watercolor rainbow over the words. Watercolor allows the words to show through.

☐ Plan a family project that connects with your faith. Examples: help at a church function, shop together to donate canned goods to a food pantry or pick up litter at church after a service.

FAMILY DEVOTION • READ ALOUD •

God's Art 2 minutes

"Look, Mom. God painted three rainbows in the big blue sky." Rebecca pointed. "I like to paint rainbows."

"Yes, you make beautiful rainbows with lots of colors."

"You read about when God painted the first rainbow. God promised Noah he wouldn't flood the whole earth again. That's in the Bible."

"Yes, rainbows remind us that God cares for all the people and creatures he made."

"I can paint big rainbows on my easel or use my colored pencils to color tiny ones on a little pad of paper. I can keep the little ones in my scrapbook."

During a two-year Coast Guard duty tour in Hawaii, Rebecca and her family watched many rainbows fill the sky with layered arcs of color. Double rainbows reversed the colors of the first one. Triple rainbows amazed them more. The third one's color order matched the first, with a bottom arch of red.

Rebecca's mom helped her make a scrapbook. She wrote in words and drew on the pages to reflect what she wanted to remember that she learned about God each day.

Bible Story Connection 3–4 minutes

Read about the rainbow in Genesis 9:13–17. Discuss how God's rainbow reminds us that God cares about us and how we should care about following God.

Chat Prompts

- *The one who sat there shone like jasper and ruby. Around the throne was a* rainbow *shining like an emerald.* Revelation 4:3 (emphasis added)

  There's a rainbow in heaven around God's throne. That's a reminder that God always recalls the promise made to Noah. How do rainbows make you feel?

- *Remember the wonderful things he has done. Remember his miracles and how he judged our enemies.* Psalm 105:5

  This verse is from a Psalm that recalls Abraham, Jacob, and Moses. It's a reminder of important Bible stories that really happened long ago. Chat about favorite Bible verses or stories and what the story means to each family member.

- *What I'm about to tell you is true. What she has done will be told anywhere the good news is preached all over the world. It will be told in memory of her.* Mark 14:9

  Jesus praised a woman that others teased for being a sinner. They thought Jesus should avoid her and not let her touch him. She washed the feet of Jesus and anointed them with perfume. Jesus praised her and said she would be remembered. She did such a small task in washing the feet of Jesus.

  Why are small tasks important to God? What little things can you do to help others?

- *Read from Genesis 1 and celebrate new beginnings. Chat about this new book of family do-votions and how you hope it will help you grow together in faith as a family.*

MORE TIME?

Scrapbook/Prayer Journal Options

Make a memory about what you read, did, and learned this week.

- Write dates and words related to memories, like birthdates and favorite times or places.

- Add the colors of the rainbow with watercolor. Write how a rainbow reminds you of God.

- Draw or trace hands of family members to commit to holding on to God and one another.

Frontline Tip

A covenant is a commitment. Write a covenant that expresses loyalty and love between the members of your family. Post it so you can remember that whether you are together or apart.

Prayer

Dear Father, thank you for putting each of us into this family. Thank you for loving us. Help our whole family stay close to you this year. In Jesus' name, amen.

Understanding a Calling

Family Beatitude: Happy is the family that understands a person's calling, for they will honor those people as heroes.

Focus: Celebrating callings

Weekly Bible Verse: *Commit to the LORD everything you do. Then he will make your plans succeed.* Proverbs 16:3

Activity Options

☐ Make a career collage of what family members do. Then make a future career collage for each child of what they might want to be when grown up. Talk about how to serve God in each chosen career.

☐ Chart each child's talents and interests. Add in the child's personality. Think of careers that fit well with each person and how the child could use their talents in serving other people.

☐ Light a candle or a fire in a fireplace. Watch the flame and use it to light another candle. Notice how easy the fire can be passed on. Talk about passing on the light of Christ. Also, talk about fire safety. Go over your family's plans in case of a home fire.

☐ Find out the history of the fire department in your area.

Called to Save Lives 2 minutes

The year was 1938 and there was a fire at St Andrew's Church. John rushed to be one of the many people who followed the smoke and smell. John and the others quickly lined up to form a bucket brigade and passed pails of water. Slowly, they were able to douse the flames, but the fire left great damage. Everyone coughed, washed their faces, and drank water to stop the smoke from stinging their eyes.

John believed the town needed their own fire department. Their town was so small they relied on another town to come and fight their fires. Of course, that often meant help arrived too late to save the homes of John's friends and relatives or the businesses the community needed.

John talked with volunteers who helped at the St Andrew's Church fire and then requested a town meeting. Even though one woman greatly objected, the vote passed! The town agreed to start a fire department and purchase a fire truck. They housed the fire truck in a barn and the town council chose John as the fire chief of the volunteer fire department.

Clang! Clang! Clang! The alarm sounded and John and his crew raced to respond. It was the house of the woman who had voted against the new fire department. They saved her house.

John served as chief for almost forty years and supervised the building of three fire stations. He believed God called him to help save lives and homes. It's hard and dangerous work to fight fires, but most firefighters feel called to help within their community and many still serve as volunteers.

Bible Story Connection 3–4 minutes

Read 1 Samuel 3 about how God called Samuel. Most people do not hear God speak to them aloud, but when we pray God answers. God gave us his Word, the Bible, to help us know what he wants us to do. As a family, talk about how the grown-ups made decisions about careers and volunteering, and talk about the future careers the kids might see for themselves.

Chat Prompts

- Read Matthew 25:14–30. This parable is about a wealthy man who gave three of his workers bags of gold to invest and use to produce more money. Two of the workers wisely doubled the money and thus were fruitful. The other one buried the gold because he was afraid he might lose it. The wealthy man praised the two who used what he gave them wisely. He scolded the one who hid the money. And took the money away from him.

    Talk about using the talents God gave you and not hiding your abilities and gifts. Ask the people in your family or community why they chose to serve.

- *God chose you to be his people. You are royal priests. You are a holy nation. You are God's special treasure. You are all these things so that you can give him praise. God brought you out of darkness into his wonderful light.* 1 Peter 2:9

    How did God make each one of your family members special? Praise God for giving you the talents that make you a treasure.

- *"I know the plans I have for you," announces the LORD. "I want you to enjoy success. I do not plan to harm you. I will give you hope for the years to come."* Jeremiah 29:11

    Pray for God to show his plans to your family. Parents, share how you chose your career and how God has blessed it.

Scrapbook/Prayer Journal Options

Make a memory about careers and serving others

- Add symbols related to careers of family members, such as fire hats or police badges.

- Write what careers children are considering now and how those careers can help others.

- Add hearts with crosses as signs that God loves you and chose you to follow him.

Frontline Tips

- Discuss the choice to serve in a more dangerous career because of God's calling.

- Make sure each child knows how to make an emergency call. Post the numbers in a place where every family member can see them.

Prayer

Dear Father, thank you for choosing us to be in your family. Guide us and help us follow the great plans you have for us. In Jesus' name, amen.

Wrap-Up

Chat about what you learned about deciding on a career and how you can find ways to serve God in any career.

Compassion

Family Beatitude: Happy is the family who has compassion, for they will develop kind hearts.

Focus: Showing concern for other people

Weekly Bible Verse: *You are God's chosen people. You are holy and dearly loved. So put on tender mercy and kindness as if they were your clothes. Don't be proud. Be gentle and patient.* Colossians 3:12

Activity Options

☐ Practice first aid of cleaning a wound and dressing it with a bandage. Try it on a doll and then a family member. Be gentle.

☐ Make a get-well card or sympathy card for someone who is ill or who has lost a loved one. Add words expressing compassion and hope for healing.

☐ Bake bread or cookies for a hurting family and give them to the family with a few kind words.

☐ Every evening, ask each person in your family how they feel, how their day went, or if something had hurt their feelings lately. Really listen and show compassion for their hurts.

Tragic News 2 minutes

Marie woke during the night to voices downstairs. She sat up and listened, Marie's grandfather and dad spoke quietly. Her grandfather, a fire chief, said, "We couldn't get there in time. I drove as fast as I could." She knew her grandfather felt sorry whenever the firefighters lost a life.

She had heard the sirens blare and trucks whiz pass the house earlier. Marie overheard her grandfather describe how a man died when his car flipped over and went up in flames. Then he said the name of the man. She froze. It was the name of her best friend's father.

Marie cried quietly as she continued listening. The police were on the way to the home to tell the family. She started praying for her best friend, her friend's sister, and their mother.

The next day, Marie helped her grandmother bake bread for her friend's family. Her friend missed several days of school, but when she came back, Marie hugged her and listened to her talk about her dad.

Marie prayed every day for her grandfather and other people who worked to save lives. She knew they cared others and that's why he chose to fight fires even though it sometimes put him in danger.

Bible Story Connection 3–4 minutes

Read Mark 8:1–9 about a time Jesus felt compassion for hungry people. Discuss how it feels to be hungry and how we can help hungry people.

26

Chat Prompts

- *A Samaritan came to the place where the man was. When he saw the man, he felt sorry for him.* Luke 10:33

  This man, called the Good Samaritan helped a man who had been robbed and beaten. He did even more than help the man. He took him to a hotel and paid the owner to continue to care for the man. The injured man belonged to a group of people who didn't like Samaritans, but the Good Samaritan felt sorry for him and responded with compassion anyway.

  Discuss noticing when someone looks hurt or needs help. Why should you help even if the person hurt was mean or didn't like you?

- *A father is tender and kind to his children. In the same way, the LORD is tender and kind to those who have respect for him.* Psalm 103:13

  Talk about hugs. How do they make you feel? How does it feel to have mom or dad kiss you and hug you when you feel hurt? Hugs are one way to show you care.

  Chat about God's love and how he cares when anyone is hurting.

- *Here is what the LORD who rules over all said to his people. "Treat everyone with justice. Show mercy and tender concern to one another."* Zechariah 7:9

  What does it mean to have tender concern? Discuss ways to show concern. Talk about how you can think of other people's needs and not just your own. Make faces and guess what they might show (joy, anger, hurt, sadness, victory).

Scrapbook/Prayer Journal Options

Add art as reminders of compassion to your scrapbook.

- Add tears with words that express compassion.
- Draw a bandage and write words of love on it.
- Draw hearts and write ways to show compassion on the hearts.

Frontline Tips

- Be ready to give big hugs to a family member who serves where there is danger (fire fighters, police, military, disaster relief workers).
- Listen if they want to talk. Understand that sometimes they don't want to talk about seeing people who got hurt or even died.

Prayer

Dear Lord, thank you for showing compassion to us. Help us to notice when someone is hurting and to reach out with kindness. In Jesus' name, amen.

Wrap-Up

Discuss what *compassion* means and ways you can show compassion to those who are hurting.

Family Mission Statement

> **Family Beatitude:** Happy is the family who knows
> their purpose, for they will be united.
>
> **Focus:** Writing a family mission statement to have a unified purpose
>
> **Weekly Bible Verse:** *Choose for yourselves right now whom you will serve.
> . . . But as for me and my family, we will serve the LORD.* Joshua 24:15

Activity Options

- ☐ Write a mission statement as a family. It can be a verse that you expand or words you choose. Write it on a poster board or notecard and hang it up or stick it on the refrigerator.

- ☐ Make a list of what your family can do to serve others together: pick up litter after church, watch children of a military family during a deployment, take a prayer walk around your block, etc. Choose from your list on a regular basis.

- ☐ Plan a family meeting. Keep it simple. Start with prayer. Ask each member to praise something done as a family. List a need or change to make. Ask each person how the family can help them. Make plans for a family outing. End with a prayer and snack.

- ☐ Make a family acrostic sign. Write a word for each letter of your family's last name that is a good quality or action to take. Frame it and hang it or make it into a sign for the door.

Daniel's Friends 2 minutes

"Come on Daniel. Let's take Jimmy and Chris for a walk." Rebecca volunteered.

"I'll read them a story when you get back." Michael said.

For several months after their mother's death, Rebecca's mom picked up the two preschool boys weekly. It gave their dad a day to focus on his business or shop for groceries. Rebecca and her whole family helped. It fit their family mission statement.

Rebecca's family had a family meeting every month to discuss how they lived their faith. One time they decided to make a family mission statement. They wrote, "We will notice when people in our church or neighborhood need help and do what we can to serve them."

When the mother of Daniel's best friend died, they helped. At first, they cooked food and brought it to them. Rebecca offered to babysit for free. She came home and said, "I think Mr. Jim needs more help than my watching the boys once in a while."

Daniel said, "I want to help, too. They could come here and play with me."

That sparked the idea to pick them up weekly for the afternoon and evening. So they've been doing that ever since.

Bible Story Connection 3–4 minutes

Read 2 Samuel 9 about David wanting to help a
son of his friend Jonathan who had died.

Chat Prompts

MORE TIME?

- *Then the family groups of Judah will say in their hearts,
  "The people of Jerusalem are strong. That's because the
  LORD who rules over all is their God."* Zechariah 12:5

    These words speak about the people of Israel. The
    strength comes from being with God. Chat about
    how your family is stronger with God, too.

- *From the Father every family in heaven and on
  earth gets its name.* Ephesians 3:15

    Chat about your family name and its origins, if known. Chat
    about why it's great that God put each person in your family.

- *I will make you into a great nation. And I will bless you. I will
  make your name great. You will be a blessing to others.* Genesis 12:2

    God gave Abraham and his family a simple purpose. He
    wanted them to bless others. Chat about how you can
    bless people and how ancestors also blessed people.

- *If any of these things has happened to you, then agree
  with one another. Have the same love. Be one in spirit
  and in the way you think and act. By doing this, you
  will make my joy complete.* Philippians 2:2

    The verse before this one talked about encouragement
    and fellowship. It's good to agree with one another
    and have some common goals. Chat about unity
    in your home. How do you create harmony?

Scrapbook/Prayer Journal Options

Add art to reflect your family's mission statement.

- Add a house and write words in it that help unite your family.

- Write the mission statement on a heart with a cross on top.

- Draw hands with hearts on them as a sign of helping others. Add text to describe or a picture to represent something your family did to help someone.

Frontline Tips

- Show appreciation for members who serve others.

- Make a thank-you card—and a hero sandwich!— for someone you know who serves others.

Prayer

Father, we thank you for our family. Help us to follow and serve you together. In Jesus' name, amen.

Wrap-Up

Celebrate your family. Take a new family photo or selfie. Chat about service you did together.

Celebrating Faithful Service

Family Beatitude: Happy is the family who celebrates service, for they will impact lives.

Focus: Honoring those who serve

Weekly Bible Verse: *What more can I say? I don't have time to tell about all the others. I don't have time to talk about Gideon, Barak, Samson and Jephthah. I don't have time to tell about David and Samuel and the prophets. Because of their faith they took over kingdoms. They ruled fairly. They received the blessings God had promised. They shut the mouths of lions. They put out great fires. They escaped being killed by swords. Their weakness was turned to strength. They became powerful in battle. They beat back armies from other countries.* Hebrews 11:32–34

Activity Options

☐ Record the deeds of family members who serve. Make a video or scrapbook page celebrating their service.

☐ Get stronger. God turned weakness to strength for these people. Strengthen your muscles with exercises. Plan different exercises to work on various muscles.

☐ Run or walk a mile to strengthen legs.

☐ Do a dozen sit-ups to build core strength.

☐ Do a few pushups for stronger arms.

- [ ] Lift weights or bottles of water to strengthen arms.
- [ ] Do stretches to help your muscles be flexible and limber.
- [ ] Do calf raises to strengthen calf muscles of your legs.
- [ ] Lie on your back and do leg raises to strengthen your core.
- [ ] Practice Fairness. Our memory verse praises people for ruling fairly.
- [ ] Choose a favorite game to play and discuss fair ways to choose who gets the first turn.
- [ ] Let one of the children divide a dessert and pass it out as fairly as they can.
- [ ] Treat someone the way you want to be treated. Do that person's chore one day or share a special toy with that individual.

FAMILY DEVOTION · READ ALOUD ·

Wall of Service 2 minutes

Two-year-old Dylan pointed to a picture on the wall and asked, "Who is that?"

Mom said, "That's your Grandpa Kyle. He is on our wall of fame. He is a missionary. He tells people in Peru about Jesus."

Dylan said, "Pray for Grandpa Kyle."

"Yes. We like to pray for the people on the wall." She said a prayer and Dylan repeated the words. Dylan then pointed to the next person. He liked the prayer wall. Every day, he led his mom or dad to the wall to name and pray for the people pictured there. They included a nurse, police officer, missionaries, and a teacher in the family. They all helped other people.

Dylan said, "Read the hall of people in Bible."

His mom smiled and read from Hebrews chapter eleven about many people from the Old Testament. They fought battles, were great leaders, and put out fires.

She said, "They sound like first responders and the military. There are people in every generation who chose to serve and help others. Moses who followed God to free the Israelites from slavery, Joseph who preserved people with storing grain, and Rahab who hid spies to keep them safe. There are many ways to serve people."

Dylan said, "I help. I pray!"

Bible Story Connection 3–4 minutes

Read about Caleb in Numbers 13:16–31 and Numbers 14:24. Moses sent Caleb and eleven other men to check out the Promised Land. These spies saw the powerful people and felt scared. Only Caleb and Joshua believed God would give them the land. Chat about how trusting God's power helps you be a faithful servant.

Chat Prompts

- *Do everything you say or do in the name of the Lord Jesus. Always give thanks to God the Father through Christ.* Colossians 3:17

  Discuss how serving your country or community is also a way to serve God. How can you do your schoolwork or other activities *for* Jesus and feel thankful for that work?

- *I am thankful to Christ Jesus our Lord. He has given me strength. I thank him that he considered me faithful. I thank him for appointing me to serve him.* 1 Timothy 1:12

  Chat about why people serve others and how God will give them strength to continue the work. Let children ask about your call to serve in your career or area of volunteering.

- *It will be good for the slave if the master finds him doing his job when the master returns.* Matthew 24:46

  Why is it important to be faithful? Why should you work even when no one is watching?

Scrapbook/Prayer Journal Options

Add art about your hall of faith or the one in Hebrews:

- Draw a wide cross and let the long upright section be a hallway to write in names of your family's heroes of faith.

- Illustrate the verse with fire, a lion, sword, and a crown.

- Draw a symbol, such as a firefighter's hat, for what you want to be when you grow up.

Frontline Tips

- Create a wall or bulletin board of fame for your family's heroes. Add a few scriptures such as 1 Timothy 1:12 or Colossians 3:17.

- Pray daily for those who are serving God and others.

Prayer

Dear Father, thanks for all our family members and other people who serve our community and country. Help us serve you as people in the Hall of Faith did. In Jesus' name, amen.

Prayer Journal

Wrap-Up

End the week by chatting about family members on your wall or bulletin board of fame. Talk about your family goal to follow God and to become a member of God's hall of fame.

Time for Family

Family Beatitude: Happy is the family that observes schedules, for they will make time for each other.

Focus: Enjoying family togetherness

Weekly Bible Verse: *Teach us to realize how short our lives are. Then our hearts will become wise.* Psalm 90:12

Activity Options

☐ Hang a large calendar for the whole family to use. Use a different pen color for each family member and fill in activities. Everyone can see who will be busy or away.

☐ Plan family time like a game night, movie night, picnic, or time at a park. Take photos.

☐ Practice how to really listen. Look the speaker in the eye and pay attention. Avoid interrupting. Give each person time to talk.

☐ Make a listening reminder: Cut out or draw a picture of an eye and an ear. Glue the eye picture to a popsicle stick. Glue the ear picture to the back of the eye picture.

Checking the Calendar 2 minutes

Robert told Drew, "Let me check the calendar." Robert was making plans to sleep over at his friend Drew's home, and wanted to check when his dad's next day off would be. Dad's homecoming was the best day of any week!

Robert's dad, a firefighter, had a rotating schedule. He had three days at work, and then three days off work. Robert didn't want to miss his dad's first day home, because that day always included a special meal, dessert, and spending time together as a family. His mom kept his dad's schedule on the calendar, so they would know where dad would be on any date.

Robert checked the calendar and told Drew, "I can sleep over on Friday but not Saturday." They checked with their moms and made plans.

Robert's dad had a schedule that made it pretty easy to plan around. Robert paused to think how not everyone had it that easy. Some moms or dads may have a more inconsistent schedule or might be away for weeks or months at a time. Robert hoped all those families got to have a very special homecoming day!

Robert eagerly waited for his dad's return that Friday night. When his dad got home, they laughed and played while his mom cooked a special meal: Dad's favorite, lasagna with garlic bread! Dad listened to what Robert did while he was away, looked at his schoolwork, and talked about the soccer game he missed. Robert was especially proud that he got to share the *A* he got on his math test. He wasn't quite so proud about the goal he missed in the game. His dad promised to spend time playing ball and helping Robert improve his aim.

Bible Story Connection 3–4 minutes

Read Ecclesiastes 3:1–8 and talk about time, routines, and plans. God says there is a time for everything and that we need a balance between work and play.

Chat Prompts

- *I remember your tears. I long to see you so that I can be filled with joy.* 2 Timothy 1:4

   Paul remembered parting from friends. He recalled their tears and feelings of sadness. Chat about the difficulty of being apart. It's natural to miss someone. Talk about what you miss when you're not together. Discuss the joy of family reunions, too.

- *Brothers and sisters, we were separated from you for a short time. Apart from you, we were like children without parents. We were no longer with you in person. But we kept you in our thoughts. We really wanted to see you. So we tried very hard to do so.* 1 Thessalonians 2:17

   Be thankful for online ways to talk face to face. Plan times to chat online. Talk about how you are together in love and spirit even when you are not physically with one another.

- *Make sure your children learn [God's commands]. Talk about them when you are at home. Talk about them when you walk along the road. Speak about them when you go to bed. And speak about them when you get up.* Deuteronomy 6:7

   Discuss why it's important to use time together to talk about God and important matters.

- *In their hearts human beings plan their lives. But the LORD decides where their steps will take them.* Proverbs 16:9

   Chat about how God guides us in life and even our careers when we pray for direction.

Scrapbook/Prayer Journal Options

Add art to express emotions about separations and reunions.

- Draw clocks and calendars to represent time. Write plans to do something together.

- Draw praying hands to remember to pray for your family, especially when you are apart. Add party hats and homecoming dates.

- Add feet to remember God guides us where we go. Remember also he wants us to spend time talking about God when we're together.

Frontline Tips

- Use an online calendar to sync time and events with all family members. Little ones can ask to see the calendar.

- Send care packages to absent family members. Those who are away from home, consider sending home a care package to your family. Let each person think of something to put in the care package.

Prayer

Lord, keep us united in love while we are apart. In Jesus' name, amen.

Wrap-Up

Discuss what you do to stay connected and how you celebrate being together.

Separation Preparations

Family Beatitude: Happy is the family that prepares for separations and reunions, for they will be hopeful.

Focus: Preparing for a family member to leave on a trip

Weekly Bible Verse: *So be very careful how you live. Do not live like people who aren't wise. Live like people who are wise. Make the most of every opportunity.* Ephesians 5:15–16

Activity Options

☐ Talk about being prepared for lonely days. Make a second separation preparedness box for the traveling family member. Fill a box with notes and cards from family members to read when the traveling family member feels lonely.

☐ Make a second separation preparedness box for the family at home. Put in photos, little games that are reminders of activities enjoyed with the absent family member, supplies to make cards, and tiny surprises.

☐ Spend time writing love notes for the traveling family member to take and have that person leave notes for each family member. These can be tucked in a lunch box, backpack, brief case, or purse.

Balloon Race 2 minutes

Jim told his family, "I'll be leaving tomorrow. You can watch the ship leave. I have a goodbye surprise so watch what happens after the ship is out in the water. When you hear the whistle blow, look at the top of the ship."

Jim had prepared a special surprise for when the ship departed. It was for his family, but also all the families who were at the departure to say good-bye to someone they love.

The morning of the ship's departure, Rebecca and Michael kissed and hugged their father, and then watched him board the ship and disappear below deck.

Rebecca asked, "Where's Daddy? I don't see him anymore."

Mommy said, "As the engineering officer, he works in the engine room below the deck."

When the ship's loud whistle blew, they looked up and saw a huge bunch of balloons rise out of one of the smoke stacks. The wind blew the balloons to shore and all the children raced to get one. Rebecca grabbed two, kept the red one, and gave the blue one to Michael as he sat in his stroller. They kept the balloons long after the air escaped.

Rebecca laughed, "Daddy filled the stack with balloons for us. It made me so happy."

Mommy smiled, "They inflated hundreds of balloons to spread joy to their families and make a special memory."

Bible Story Connection 3–4 minutes

Read. 2 Samuel 6:12–15. When David returned from his military service the people celebrated with a parade and shouting. They won a big battle and recovered the Ark of the Covenant. That's a special box of gold built to hold the Ten Commandments, a jar of manna, and Aaron's rod (Hebrews 9:4). Talk about how you celebrate reunions.

Chat Prompts

- *Don't hold back good from those who are worthy of it. Don't hold it back when you can help.* Proverbs 3:27

    Proverbs are wise thoughts of good choices. This verse comes from a section on kindness. Kindness shows you care. Kind words help a person feel valued (worthy). Talk about how to be kind to one another in words and actions.

- *Scripture says, "Honor your father and mother." That is the first commandment that has a promise.* Ephesians 6:2

    The next verse in Ephesians (verse 3) is a reminder that things will go well for those who keep the command to obey their parents. Chat about how life is easier when rules are followed.

    Chat about obeying the parent at home and how the absence of a family member will go more smoothly as everyone is supportive and follows the rules.

- *We are God's creation. He created us to belong to Christ Jesus. Now we can do good works. Long ago God prepared these works for us to do.* Ephesians 2:10

    Chat about the importance of the work of the family member who serves and the need to make the world a better place. What good things can other family members do to help others?

MORE TIME?

43

Scrapbook/Prayer Journal Options

Fill the page with love notes and reminders to review during the days spent apart.

- Add hearts with notes in them.

- Draw a clock with arms set to a time when everyone will stop what they are doing to pray for the family.

- Draw a sun to recall that you are under the same sun while apart.

Frontline Tips

- Plan family time before a deployment or other time of separation. Let it include snuggling and sharing memories. Talk about how you'll stay in touch and will think of one another.

- Do a home inspection before the family member leaves on a trip or deployment. This is especially important if the family member is the one who usually completes home repairs. Complete any needed repairs with the help of all family members.

- Stand outside and look at the sun together. Chat about how each day you are under the same sun and share the warmth of the same love. Hold hands and pray together.

Prayer

Lord, help us treasure our time together and prepare our hearts for the days apart. In Jesus' name, amen.

Wrap-Up

Talk about any upcoming days apart and ways to feel connected.

Protection

Family Beatitude: Happy is the family who protects their children, for they will feel safe.

Focus: Providing protection to help family members feel secure

Weekly Bible Verse: *By wisdom a house is built. Through understanding it is made secure.* Proverbs 24:3

Activity Options

- ☐ Play I Spy when outside or in unfamiliar surroundings to help children become aware or their environment and possible strangers.

- ☐ Use the buddy system when you take walks.

- ☐ Practice safe ways to answer the door and phone.

Playing it Safe 2 minutes

Kathy asked Valerie, "How do you protect your children?"

Valerie replied, "With Douglas being a police officer, we set up safety rules. We always lock our doors. If the children play outside, the dog goes out with them. We taught them to look around, notice their surroundings, and come back inside if they see strangers."

Kathy replied, "I need to do those things, too. What else do you do?"

"Douglas parks his police car in the garage, so we don't advertise that he's a police officer. As he drives home he always notices cars he doesn't recognize, and he looks for anything unusual. However, he calls the local police station to report anything suspicious, rather than take matters into his own hands. With all his training, he's naturally observant and careful! It took me a while to get used to that."

Kathy said, "We discuss escape routes at home and school."

Valerie's daughter said, "We did that. Dad told us to trust our gut and if I feel worried, I should come inside or call."

Valerie added, "I never tutor at home. I meet clients in safe places like coffee shops and libraries. We have initials and not our names printed on checks. Our son Larry started driving, so he checks in with us, so we know his plans and location. It's all normal for us."

Kathy said, "I know you're very close. You talk about everything. That's what I want."

Bible Story Connection 3–4 minutes

Read Acts 27:39–44 about how a leader realized evil plans to kill Paul and others, so he kept them safe. Discuss how you protect your children from harm.

Chat Prompts

MORE TIME?

- *[Love] always protects. It always trusts. It always hopes. It never gives up.* 1 Corinthians 13:7

   Chat about why parents set rules and how those rules show love.

- *David spoke about him. He said, "I know that the Lord is always with me. Because he is at my right hand, I will always be secure."* Acts 2:25

   Discuss God's care and how he is always with each person.

- *Wise people see danger and go to a safe place. But childish people keep going and suffer for it.* Proverbs 22:3

   Chat about making wise choices to stay safe.

Scrapbook/Prayer Journal Options

Create a memory page about protecting one another.

- Draw an eye and write about being observant.

- Draw a key and write about locks and locking doors.

- Draw a heart and write about how your family protects one another.

Frontline Tips

- Discuss how a parent's career might make your family more aware of safety.

- Talk about the difficulties of being part of a police or law enforcement family and how some people don't like police.

Prayer

Father, thank you for protecting us and always watching us. In Jesus' name, amen.

Wrap-Up

Chat about one safety rule that your family always follows.

Cherished

> **Family Beatitude:** Happy is the family who knows they are cherished by God.
>
> **Focus:** Knowing God cherishes us and always watches over us.
>
> **Weekly Bible Verse:** *No one ever hated their own body. Instead, they feed and care for their body. And this is what Christ does for the church.* Ephesians 5:29

Activity Options

The following activities all involve apples. The idea is that apples can be reminders that God cherishes us. In other words, we're the "apple of his eye."

Apple Experiment: Dancing Apple Seeds

☐ Stir one teaspoon baking soda into ½ cup water. Drop in apple seeds. Add 1 teaspoon lemon juice. Watch the seeds dance in the mixture. The chemical reaction of the base (baking soda) and acid (lemon juice) causes bubbles. The bubbles lift the light seeds. Talk about the reaction of God's love that makes your heart happy.

Apple Art

☐ Cut apples crosswise, dip in paint and press onto paper to make apple prints.

☐ Use a toothpick to poke holes in an apple. Stick cloves in the holes to make a sweet smelling pomander.

Apple Games

☐ Have apple rolling contests to see who can roll the apple the farthest.

☐ Bob for apples. Place apples in a basin of water, dunk in and grab one with your teeth. They float because an apple is up to eighteen percent air.

Apple Cooking

☐ Peel, core, and slice one apple. Put slices in a microwave-safe bowl. Sprinkle sugar and ground cinnamon or apple pie spice on the apple slices. Microwave for two minutes (less if using a soft apple). Cook thirty seconds more if needed.

Apple Picking

☐ Go apple picking if there's an apple orchard nearby. Check out all the types of apples at the store and try different types. About 2500 kinds of apples grow in the U.S.

FAMILY DEVOTION • READ ALOUD •

Cherished 2 minutes

"Mom, may I have an apple?" Tilly asked.

"Yes, we have apples, thanks to the food program."

"Apples taste so good. I like them better than the canned food.

"Honey, we don't have much money, so we need to be thankful for all the food people donate so we and others don't go hungry. Even the canned meat! I helped as a volunteer last week, so another volunteer gave me her bag of apples and we have plenty." She cut an apple in half crosswise and gave it to Tilly.

"I see the star the seeds make like you showed me. I'm happy God made apples."

"Yes, God put that star there for us. You're the apple of his eye."

Tilly laughed. Her mom explained about the apple of God's eye.

She said, "Hebrew has four words for apple. One word is *ishon* and it refers to the pupil or the eye. Come close and look at me. We see one another and everything else is out of your eyesight. God focuses on you like that. He loves to gaze at you! He cherishes you."

Tilly and her mom thank God in prayer every day for the Society of St. Andrew and the farmers who partner with them to fulfill their motto, "Gleaning America's Fields." The Society of St. Andrew volunteers collect unsold food that would otherwise go to waste, and distribute the food to families in need.

Bible Story Connection 3–4 minutes

Read Matthew 25:35–40 where Jesus talks about the importance of helping other people.

Chat Prompts

- *The right ruling at the right time is like golden apples in silver jewelry.* Proverbs 25:11

    This verse creates a pretty picture. What words can you say to paint a word picture? Try complimenting one another with pretty words.

- *Through us, God spreads the knowledge of Christ everywhere like perfume.* 2 Corinthians 2:14

    Another Hebrew word for apple is tappuwach. It refers to fragrance, so it means to be a sweet scent. The root word means to scatter or blow. How does apple pie smell? Chat about being a sweet scent that scatters seeds of kindness.

MORE TIME?

- *The fruit the Holy Spirit produces is love, joy and peace. It is being patient, kind and good. It is being faithful and gentle and having control of oneself.* Galatians 5:22-23

  Chat about ways to encourage the fruit of the Spirit to grow in the lives of your family members.

- *In the same way, every good tree bears good fruit. But a bad tree bears bad fruit.* Matthew 7:17

  Discuss fruitful trees and how we can be fruitful.

Scrapbook/Prayer Journal Options

Add art to celebrate being the apple of God's eye:

- Do an apple print on the page.

- Draw a tree with apples. On the apples write deeds you can do to show good fruit.

Frontline Tips

- Find out about groups who help the hungry in your community. Thank them for their work.

- Volunteer to help if you can. Be sure you are healthy when you volunteer.

Prayer

Almighty God, thanks for keeping each of us in the apple of your eye and cherishing us. Help us to cherish you. In Jesus' name, amen.

Wrap-Up

Discuss activities tried and what everyone enjoys about apples and how apples can remind us that God cherishes us.

Support Network

Family Beatitude: Happy is the family that accepts help gratefully, for they will be supported.

Focus: Accepting outside support

Weekly Bible Verse: *If you love one another, everyone will know you are my disciples.* John 13:35

Activity Options

☐ Look at a support beam in your home and chat about how it provides strength to keep your home secure. Supporting people is also important. Offer support to others when a family member has to be away from home. Consider babysitting, helping with yard work, or fixing them a meal.

☐ Post a list of contacts to call for assistance when a parent or guardian is away. It's good for the departing parent or guardian to ask neighbors or friends to lend additional support to their family.

☐ Thank supporters. Make a snack, invite them over for a gratitude party, and/or send thank-you cards.

Yard Cleanup 2 minutes

A noise outside startled everyone. Darlene looked out and said, "Hey, Hank is here with a bunch of people. They're mowing the lawn."

Sure enough, a group of youth and one leader had started mowing, trimming edges, and even weeding the garden. Darlene and her mother walked outside.

Hank walked over and said, "I told your husband I'd help out if you needed anything. I noticed the lawn needed cutting and rounded up some helpers."

Darlene's dad had asked people at Bible study if anyone was willing to be called if his family needed help after he deployed. Hank and others agreed. But they went a little further. They drove by the house to see if they could do extra things without being asked. Their wives also called to see what the family needed. They wanted to be supportive.

Darlene's mom smiled. The surprise made her day. She offered drinks and snacks to the volunteers and her family enjoyed the company.

Hank hugged Darlene and her brother before he left. Darlene said, "I love this kind of surprise. I miss Daddy, but I'm happy we have helpful friends."

Bible Story Connection 3–4 minutes

Read about gleaning in Ruth 2. God told the Israelites to let poor people collect the leftovers from the harvest. It's called *gleaning*. It provided a way for poor people to work for food and not need to beg.

Chat Prompts

MORE TIME?

● *In everything I did, I showed you that we must work hard and help the weak. We must remember the words of the Lord Jesus. He said, "It is more blessed to give than to receive."* Acts 20:35

> We need help with different tasks. How can your family support others who have an absent parent? How do you feel when you help another family?

● *None of you should look out just for your own good. Each of you should also look out for the good of others.* Philippians 2:4

> It's easy to whine and want things. It's harder to think about how someone else feels or what the person may need. Chat about your church family and other groups.
>
> How do they provide support? How do they look out for you? What do you do to look out for other people, including family members? How can even kind and encouraging words help?

● *Let us consider how we can stir up one another to love. Let us help one another to do good works.* Hebrews 10:24

> Talk about making cookies with a recipe. You stir the ingredients together to blend them and to make something that tastes better than just eating the flour, eggs, and sugar separately. Blending and working together is like that. It creates loving actions.
>
> How can your family members support one another?
>
> Can your family start or help a church ministry to support families of first responders and the military?

Scrapbook/Prayer Journal Options

Add notes and art to show support received.

- Draw a hand. Write in names of anyone who supports your family, especially during deployments.

- Draw a support beam and write a prayer on it, thanking God for his support.

- Draw a church and write how people at church help your family and how you help them.

Frontline Tips

- If you know military families or other families where a parent or guardian needs to travel for extended times, offer to be part of their support team.

- Do more than asked for. Drive or stop by to find out how a family in need is really doing. Notice what you can do and then offer to do it.

Prayer

Lord, thanks for giving us strength and support when we are separated. Help us be grateful for all support we receive. In Jesus' name, amen.

Wrap-Up

As a family, hold hands and chat about how you learned more about support this week. Let each person share what encouraged or helped them.

Teamwork

Family Beatitude: Happy is the family that overcomes problems together, for they will form a strong team.

Focus: Working together, especially during hard times

Weekly Bible Verse: *[Jesus] got up and ordered the wind to stop. He said to the waves, "Quiet! Be still!" Then the wind died down. And it was completely calm.* Mark 4:39

Activity Options

☐ Make a volcano with baking soda and vinegar. Add food coloring. Watch it bubble over and make a mess. It's a chemical reaction that reflects the power of nature. Problems can seem to explode and be overwhelming at times, but storms end and so can problems.

☐ Make a home emergency kit. The contents may vary depending on the type of problems that occur where you live. Most will have first aid items, flashlight and batteries, radio and batteries, water, and canned foods with easy-to-open lids.

☐ Plan a family project that takes teamwork, like painting a room or planning a picnic. Discuss how everyone can help. Take photos.

Troubled Winds 2 minutes

The news grew worse. A major hurricane was headed their way. The girls started baking bread and filling every container with water. The boys started hauling in bikes, toys, and furniture from outside.

Karen thought, *Once again, my husband's away on military orders when trouble strikes.* Karen grabbed two-year-old Daniel and headed for the store to buy provisions. Once home, she spoke with her husband, Jim, by phone. He gave some advice and prayed with her, but he knew he couldn't return to Florida before the hurricane hit.

The people in their zip code received word to remain home and keep the highways available for people leaving more endangered areas. They lost power before the hurricane turned directly into their town. By ten o'clock that night, Karen watched huge gumbo-limbo trees behind the house bend in half.

Fifteen-year-old Rebecca helped her finish tying doors closed and then rushed downstairs. They joined the other children sleeping on mattresses in the basement. Crashing sounds and howling wind continued all night.

During the times of waking, Karen read from the Bible and prayed. At about five or six o'clock the next morning, she read about Jesus walking on water. She prayed for Jesus to stop the storm. Everything quieted.

After two minutes of silence, Michael piped up, "Mom, you should have read that one first." Everyone laughed before checking the damage and cleaning the debris.

Bible Story Connection 3–4 minutes

Read Mark 4:35–41 about Jesus calming the storm. Discuss the disciples' fear and how storms and other things are dangerous. Talk about how Jesus can help us be calm.

Chat Prompts

MORE TIME?

- *The Holy Spirit is given to each of us in a special way. That is for the good of all.* 1 Corinthians 12:7

  Talk about the strengths of each family member. How can they use their strengths to cooperate in family life?

- *I have told you these things, so that you can have peace because of me. In this world you will have trouble. But be encouraged! I have won the battle over the world.* John 16:33

  Life can be tough. Jesus mentioned that we will have problems, but he told us to have hope and not let the problems discourage us. He knows the end result will be great.

  After a problem is resolved, chat about it and find the lighter side of lessons learned. Discuss what brought hope and helped you continue to work through the problem.

- *You must allow this strength to finish its work. Then you will be all you should be. You will have everything you need.* James 1:4

  Some deployments are longer than others. Talk about how to keep going while waiting for the parent's return. Chat about how everyone grew stronger in getting through a long separation or a hard time.

Scrapbook/Prayer Journal Options

Add art about the hard times.

- Draw a whirlwind or gray cloud. Add words about problems you or your family faced.

- Write out and decorate the verse that is most helpful to you in hard times.

- Draw arm muscles with hearts and write ways you are stronger because of problems you overcame.

Frontline Tips

- Hold an emergency drill.

- Post numbers to call in case of emergencies.

Prayer

Dear Lord, you can calm any storm or heart. Help us to be calm during difficulties and to work together to solve problems. In Jesus' name, amen.

Wrap-Up

Talk about how you might face the next big problem better because of what you learned this week.

Shared Laughter

Family Beatitude: Happy is the family that laughs together, for they will know joy.

Focus: Uniting through shared laughter

Weekly Bible Verse: *There is a time to weep. And there's a time to laugh. There is a time to be sad. And there's a time to dance.* Ecclesiastes 3:4

Activity Options

- ☐ Check out library books with jokes or humor or purchase a few at your local bookstore.

- ☐ Tell stories from your childhood that will amuse your children. Start a laugh journal to remember what made your family members laugh. Record funny incidents that happen and humorous phrases people in your family say.

- ☐ Make faces and see who laughs first. What else do you do to encourage laughter?

Doused 2 minutes

Jim waltzed in three days after a major hurricane and jokingly asked, "Anything unusual happen while I was gone?"

"Well," I replied, "Daniel learned three new words, 'Hur'cain did it!'"

By then Jim had crossed the room, pulled me into his arms, and said, "I'm so sorry I wasn't here. I thought I'd never get a flight home." He held up his suitcase and continued, "My treasure chest is full of cash, batteries, and emergency supplies."

He praised the children's hard work including bailing out the living room and removing soaked carpeting. He laughed with them as they shared crazy things like a tiny picture that was left on the wall when everything else in the room had crashed down! We all joked that our missing paper plates must have flown out like flying saucers when the doors blew open.

It took months for the $99,000 in repairs to be completed. For the first few weeks, every time Jim reached for a glass, he doused himself with water. He'd forget that our daughters had filled every container with water, including every glass and bowl. Everyone else slid the glasses out carefully, remembering they might hold water. The children chorused, "Gotcha again! You should've been here. Then, you'd remember the water."

Bible Story Connection 3–4 minutes

Read Matthew 17:24–27 and discover how Jesus solved a problem with an answer that might seem silly and could make you laugh.

Chat Prompts

- *He will fill your mouth with laughter. Shouts of joy will come from your lips.* Job 8:21

  Job had a really hard time. All his children died. He lost all his animals on his farm and all his crops. It all happened in one day. But, his friend Bildad spoke and said that God would fill his mouth with laughter. That's faith!

  How does it help in hard times to know God will give you a better future? Chat about what makes each person laugh.

- *Here is what I am commanding you to do. Be strong and brave. Do not be afraid. Do not lose hope. I am the LORD your God. I will be with you everywhere you go.* Joshua 1:9

  God spoke to Joshua before the Israelites entered the Promised Land. God didn't promise an easy time. They would face struggles. Even so, God wanted them to remember that he would be with them. Does it help to see how God helped his people? When has God helped your family?

- *Then young women will dance and be glad. And so will the men, young and old alike. I will turn their mourning into gladness. I will comfort them. And I will give them joy instead of sorrow.* Jeremiah 31:13

  Jeremiah is sometimes called the weeping prophet. He preached about hard times ahead. The people persecuted Jeremiah because they didn't like the messages God sent. God also gave Jeremiah some good news about the future to give the people hope.

  Problems can turn into something good. When has a hard time become a blessing?

Scrapbook/Prayer Journal Options

Add art and notes about laughter.

- Add smiles and jokes that made someone laugh.

- Draw a cartoon of something that is funnier now that it was when it happened.

- Add funny faces and happy thoughts.

Frontline Tips

- Life serving others can be tough, so we need laughter. Find and bookmark good joke sites online.

- Record memories that make everyone laugh.

Prayer

Dear Lord, thanks for helping us get through hard times. Help us find the lighter side of past troubles. In Jesus' name, amen.

Wrap-Up

Talk about how it's much easier to talk about a past problem than it was to live through it. Talk about ways to get through other problems by remembering that tough times will pass.

Care Packages

Family Beatitude: Happy is the family who gives gifts to one another, for they will be caring.

Focus: Showing we care for one another

Weekly Bible Verse: *[Joseph] sent his father ten male donkeys loaded with the best things from Egypt. He also sent ten female donkeys loaded with grain and bread and other supplies for his journey.* Genesis 45:23

Activity Options

☐ Prepare a care package for someone. Think of items that will be meaningful, like ones related to shared interests or activities. Add little pompoms as reminders you are cheering for the person to do well.

☐ Hang a map for children to see where the absent family member will travel. Add the night sky map.

☐ Take photos made when the whole family is together. These make great gifts to bridge distances. Frame the pictures for the children to have beside their beds.

Care Package 2 minutes

"Mommy, I have something to send in Daddy's care package. You need to write the note."

Rebecca handed me a cup and saucer from her toy tea set. She dictated how she missed having tea parties with her daddy. She said that she wanted him to pretend they were together for tea and she'd do the same.

Rebecca ran off to her room and started an imaginary conversation with her dad. She giggled and gave him an *airwhich,* made of two slices of air with a breeze for the filling. It was one of their little treats they laughed about. Her gray stuffed seal named *Tall* sat next to her. Her very tall daddy gave her the seal when he returned from a fishery patrol in Alaska.

With each care package we sent, we also made recordings to send. In turn, Jim sent us recordings with all the noises of the ship in the background.

In the Old Testament, Joseph had not seen his father in years. When he reunited with his brothers and they returned to their father, Joseph sent large care packages of wagons filled with clothes, food, and other gifts. He wanted to give gifts his father who had long ago given him a very special, colorful coat (Genesis 37:3).

Tangible gifts express care and love, bridging the distance of separations.

Bible Story Connection 3–4 minutes

Esther 9:19–22 is about a time Jews celebrated and sent gifts to one another. They sent gift of food and also gifts for the poor. Talk about how we give gifts as part of celebrations to share joy.

Chat Prompts

MORE TIME?

- *One day Elisha went to the town of Shunem. A rich woman lived there. She begged him to stay and have a meal. So every time he came by, he stopped there to eat.* 2 Kings 4:8

  This woman first gave a traveling prophet a meal. Later she and her husband made a guest room for him to stay when he visited. Chat about gifts you can make for others and ways to serve them. Chat about how you treat visitors.

- *He takes care of his flock like a shepherd. He gathers the lambs in his arms. He carries them close to his heart. He gently leads those that have little ones.* Isaiah 40:11

  Jesus cares for us. He is called the Good Shepherd. This verse describes some of the care a shepherd gives his little lambs. Discuss ways Jesus cares for his little lambs. What gifts and blessings does Jesus give you?

- *I needed clothes. And you gave them to me. I was sick. And you took care of me. I was in prison. And you came to visit me.* Matthew 25:36

  God wants us to care for other people, including ones in need. Jesus used these words and more in the same chapter of Matthew to talk about ways to care for people. He said that when we take care of someone we are also taking care of him.

  Chat about ways to care for needy people. Choose one idea and carry it out.

Scrapbook/Prayer Journal Options

Add art to show the importance of little gifts and thoughtful deeds.

- Draw bows and packages. Add notes of special gifts you have given.

- Draw items sent in a care package.

- Write heart notes with messages inside hearts that express your love to a family member who has to be away at times.

Frontline Tips

- Before a deployment, let the departing family member create a small care package for each other family member. Pass them out when everyone seems to really miss the absent person.

- After a family member deploys, set aside a day and time to create a care package weekly and fill it with cheerful notes, baked goodies, and small mementos.

Prayer

Dear Father, we thank you for the time our family is together. Help us stay close when we are apart. In Jesus' name, amen.

Wrap-Up

Talk about what makes a gift or care package special.

Comfort

Family Beatitude: Happy is the family that comforts others, for they will be considerate.

Focus: Lessening fear and worry

Weekly Bible Verse: *I was very worried. But your comfort brought me joy.* Psalm 94:19

Activity Options

- [ ] Enjoy a group hug with everyone in the family. Have group hugs often.

- [ ] As a family, practice activities that lessen stress, fear, and worry:
  - ○ Take several slow breaths
  - ○ Count to ten or tap each finger
  - ○ Jog or walk in place
  - ○ Stop and look outside at nature
  - ○ Laugh together!

- [ ] Hobbies help relieve stress. Talk about hobbies family members enjoy and let children try a few hobbies to discover what they can do to relax.

- [ ] Have a teddy bear picnic to celebrate teddy bears and hugs. Cut out a paper teddy bear with arms open wide. Fold in the arms and give it to someone to give them a teddy bear hug.

Teddy Bears to the Rescue!

2 minutes

"Daddy is that Smokey the Bear?" the little girl asked her firefighter father. She pointed to a teddy bear sitting on the dashboard of the fire truck.

"No, that's one of our rescue bears."

"Do the bears put out the fires?"

"No. But when we rescue a girl or boy, they are often scared. Some cry or shake while others are too scared to move. We give them a bear to hold and that usually makes them smile and feel better. The bear helps stop the tears."

"Oh, teddy bears to the rescue!" She hugged her daddy.

Her daddy smiled and said, "Yes. Thanks, I needed a hug."

You might see a teddy bear on the dashboard of a police car or fire truck. Children hug the fuzzy stuffed animals and feel better. Hugs Across America is an organization that raises funds for bears for children who need comfort after a fire or accident.

You may have a stuffed animal or real pet you hug. Hugs bring comfort. When your mom and dad work hard all day they need a hug, too.

Bible Story Connection 3–4 minutes

Read Genesis 46:28–29 about the reunion between Joseph and his father. Talk about how they cried and hugged. Talk about your reunions.

Chat Prompts

- *They all wept as they hugged and kissed him.* Acts 20:37

    When Paul said goodbye to friends in Ephesus, they cried, hugged, and prayed together.

    Talk about the comfort of a good hug. Make sure to pray together before you go different ways. Each morning as a family, you can pray for God to keep everyone in your family safe.

- *Even though I walk through the darkest valley, I will not be afraid. You are with me. Your shepherd's rod and staff comfort me.* Psalm 23:4

    This is a line from Psalm 23. It describes God as a person's shepherd. In the same way sheep trust their shepherd's care, we should trust God to care for us.

    How is God like a shepherd? How can remembering these words and other Bible verses help you when you feel afraid or sad? Chat about how it is helpful to memorize Scripture. Verses bring comfort when you're afraid. Try memorizing this one as a family.

- *Your love has given me great joy. It has encouraged me. My brother, you have renewed the hearts of the Lord's people.* Philemon 1:7

    Paul wrote these words about how his friends encouraged and comforted him. Ask each person in your family what brings them the most comfort. How do you thank people who show you love and encourage you?

71

Scrapbook/Prayer Journal Options

Add artwork as reminders of comfort.

- Draw teddy bears on the pages.

- Draw a shepherd and sheep. Write that God cares for you.

- Write notes of what brings you comfort and favorite Bible verses.

- Draw symbols of what helps lessen fear and stress.

Frontline Tips

- Agree to send hugs when you are apart. Go outside wrap your arms around yourself and open them up to send a hug. Catch one by extending arms and then closing them around your shoulders.

- Consider getting a soldier doll or special stuffed animal for your child to cuddle during times of fear or separation.

Prayer

Dear Lord, comfort us when we feel afraid or worried. Help us to comfort others. Keep our family members safe, especially when we are apart. In Jesus' name, amen.

Wrap-Up

Chat about the importance of comfort and how teddy bears and hugs bring comfort. Chat about praying for one another.

Lifelines

Family Beatitude: Happy is the family who seek help for they will find a lifeline.

Focus: Helping in emergencies

Weekly Bible Verse: *Ask, and it will be given to you. Search, and you will find. Knock, and the door will be opened to you.* Matthew 7:7

Activity Options

☐ Practice with children on what to say if they need to call 9-1-1. Make and post a 9-1-1 prompt card on what to say, their address, phone number, how to describe the emergency (fire, medical, burglary), and who is involved. They should be told it's safe to give that person who answers their address. Make sure they understand when to make such calls.

☐ 9-1-1 calls began in 1968. Use the internet to find out about the history of 9-1-1 calls.

☐ Practice emergency response for choking and watch a video on the new way to do CPR (cardiopulmonary resuscitation).

My Dad's in Trouble 2 minutes

"Hello this is 9-1-1. What's your emergency?"

Unseen, Duane nodded.

"Hello, don't be afraid. Just let me know what's wrong."

"It's my dad."

"Thank you for speaking up. What's your name and where do you live?"

"Duane." He gave his address.

"You're doing great Duane. Tell me what is wrong with your dad."

"He has cancer and fell down. He's shaking and swinging his arms. It's a . . . a seashore."

"He's having a seizure. Has he had them before?"

"Yes. I prayed and remembered to call 9-1-1."

"That's good. Stay on the phone until the ambulance arrives. Let me know when they get there."

The emergency responder spoke softly to Duane until the EMTs had arrived.

An EMT checked out the father while another one talked to Duane and helped him understand what they were doing. The seizure ended, but they took him to the hospital and Duane rode with his dad and stayed at the hospital until a family member arrived to pick him up.

Bible Story Connection 3–4 minutes

Read how Jesus calmly responded to an emergency
when Jairus pleaded for help, in Mark 5:21–43.

Chat Prompts

- *So do not be afraid. I am with you. Do not be terrified. I am
  your God. I will make you strong and help you. I will hold you
  safe in my hands. I always do what is right.* Isaiah 41:10

   How do these words help you feel safe? How can
   you say them as a prayer when you are afraid?
   What is the difference between God doing what
   we want and us following God's plans?

- *I have told you these things, so that you can have peace
  because of me. In this world you will have trouble. But be
  encouraged! I have won the battle over the world.* John 16:33

   Discuss how Jesus knows we will have trouble. How
   can that help us remain calm during emergencies?

- *A friend loves at all times. They are there to help
  when trouble comes.* Proverbs 17:17

   How can we help one another in trouble? How are EMTs,
   firefighters, police, and other responders our friends?

Scrapbook/Prayer Journal Options

Use art to share about staying calm in emergencies

- Draw a police car, fire truck, or ambulance and write about people who help in emergencies.

- Draw a phone and write what you might need to tell someone if you call 9-1-1.

- Add a heart and write what will help you not be afraid.

Frontline Tips

- When EMTs and other rescue people arrive, be sure to stay out of the way.

- Thank the EMTS who helped.

Prayer

Dear Father, we trust you even when we are afraid. Help us be calm in emergencies. In Jesus' name, amen.

Wrap-Up

Chat about when to call 9-1-1.

Gratitude

Family Beatitude: Happy is the family who expresses gratitude, for they will be optimistic.

Focus: Being thankful

Weekly Bible Verse: *When one of [the lepers] saw that he was healed, he came back. He praised God in a loud voice.* Luke 17:15

Activity Options

☐ Choose an evening to light a candle and sit around it as a family. Talk about how the light glows and we can bring glowing smiles to people when we remember to give them thanks. Ask each person to name one thing for which they are grateful to God.

☐ Write letters of gratitude to anyone who blessed or lent a helping hand to a family member. Make this a regular habit.

☐ Cut hearts (or fold paper accordion style to cut a row of hearts). Write thanks on each one. Add thoughtful sentiments like "Your kindness brightened my day." Hand them to people to express thanks for any act of kindness—big or small!

Saved, Saving Others 2 minutes

Six-year-old Anissa woke up feeling hot. Her mother threw a quilt over her head and told her to keep it there. She stood still with fear, hardly able to breathe. Minutes later a firefighter named Steve scooped her up and carried her to safety.

The fire started in the kitchen and spread until thick smoke filled the entire New York City apartment. Ladder Company 33 responded. She lost her dad in the fire, but the firefighters saved her mother. Anissa and her mother suffered burns and smoke-filled lungs. Anissa spent time in the hospital recovering.

Anissa felt so thankful to Firefighter Steve and the other firefighters who saved her and her mom that she decided to become a firefighter when she grew up. She studied hard in school. She also read all she could about fire safety and firefighters.

Sixteen years later, Anissa graduated from firefighter school in Florida. She never forgot her hero, Firefighter Steve. Once she became a firefighter, she visited him to thank him. Steve and his buddies at the New York City fire station rejoiced to see her grown up and making great choices after her childhood rescue and trauma. In big cities, like New York, firefighters seldom see people they rescued, but they remember them.

Bible Story Connection 3–4 minutes

Read Acts 28:1–10 about Paul healing people on an island and how they responded to show their gratitude. In this story you'll also see that the people helped Paul and his friends after a shipwreck.

Chat Prompts

MORE TIME?

- *Give thanks no matter what happens. God wants you to thank him because you believe in Christ Jesus.* 1 Thessalonians 5:18

  Chat about what this verse means and how we can be thankful even when we are hurting.

- *Give thanks as you enter the gates of his temple. Give praise as you enter its courtyards. Give thanks to him and praise his name.* Psalm 100:4

  Discuss an attitude of thanksgiving. How does your family enter church? What are you usually feeling?

- *Jesus touched [Peter's mother-in-law's] hand, and the fever left her. She got up and began to serve him.* Matthew 8:15

  Talk about how our actions also express gratitude. What did this woman do after being healed?

Scrapbook/Prayer Journal Options

Create memories about family members who help others.

- Draw praying hands and write words of thanks on them.

- Draw symbols for different careers. Write how people in those careers can help people.

- Put a bandage on the page and write about a time God healed you or someone you love.

Frontline Tips

- Thank workers or volunteers who help in your church or community.

Prayer

Thank you, Father, for all the community servers we have. Bless their families and help them know you appreciate them. In Jesus' name, amen.

Wrap-Up

Chat about how the career of family members and how they help people.

Feeding Hungry Neighbors

Week 17

Family Beatitude: Happy is the family who helps their neighbors, for they will build a strong community.

Focus: Feeding the hungry near you

Weekly Bible Verse: *Jesus took the loaves and gave thanks. He handed out the bread to those who were seated. He gave them as much as they wanted. And he did the same with the fish.* John 6:11

Activity Options

- ☐ Make bread or other food to give to a neighbor.

- ☐ Collect food to give to a food pantry. If your church doesn't have a collection box for feeding the hungry, see if you can start one.

- ☐ Check to find out if you can take food to a park or a shelter to feed the homeless. Make and take sandwiches or try to buy or make a complete and nutritious meal from food in cans and boxes. Do this as a family, or start a group of families to serve in this way on a regular basis.

81

Bread Bank 2 minutes

Bria put on her hair net and slid fingers of one hand into a latex glove and then did the same with her other hand. She picked up a large bag of unwrapped loaves of bread from a local bakery. She packed each loaf. She set aside a tomato basil loaf for the old man down the street.

"Mom, they had tomato basil. Can I take it to our neighbor?"

Bria's mom, Beth, smiled, "Sure. You always remember he likes it."

At the age of ten, Bria started helping with the bread bank ministry that her parents ran. Now as a teen she still enjoyed being a part of it. Bria knew this was one of the only fresh-food ministries for hungry people in Philadelphia. They passed out bread to people in need at their church and in the community. They also shared the extra bread with other churches that distributed to needy people in their areas. After a while, the grocery and bakery that made donations added a second day of supplying leftovers. As a result, they were able to expand the ministry to another church that held services midweek.

Bria stacked the bags of bread in boxes and got them ready to go.

Beth said, "Honey, you are such a big help."

Bria said, "Mom. I know you and Dad love feeding people and I do, too."

Bible Story Connection 3–4 minutes

Read Mark 8:1–10 about Jesus feeding a crowd of people and how he felt about their hunger.

Chat Prompts

MORE TIME?

- *I feel deep concern for these people. They have already been with me three days. They don't have anything to eat.* Mark 8:2

  How do you feel about the hungry? When have you felt hungry? Imagine going a day or two without food.

- *Jesus said, "I am the bread of life. Whoever comes to me will never go hungry. And whoever believes in me will never be thirsty."* John 6:35

  Chat about what it means that Jesus is the bread of life. Why is spiritual food more important than food we eat?

- *Blessed are those who are hungry and thirsty for what is right. They will be filled.* Matthew 5:6

  What kind of hunger is described here? How can we help people who need justice?

Scrapbook/Prayer Journal Options

Show the fun of eating together.

- Draw bread on the pages and write on one that Jesus is the Bread of Life.

- Draw foods that are healthy for people.

- Draw ingredients that are used to make bread.

Frontline Tips

When donating to a food bank add notes to thank the volunteers. If they work with fresh food, include some hair nets and gloves.

Prayer

Thank you, Father, for food that fills our tummies. Help us to share what we have and give food to the needy. In Jesus' name, amen.

Wrap-Up

Chat about why feeding the hungry is a ministry.

Trusted Community Workers

Family Beatitude: Happy is the family with trusted community workers, for they will know peace.

Focus: Trusting community helpers

Weekly Bible Verse: *Suppose you can be trusted with something very little. Then you can also be trusted with something very large. But suppose you are not honest with something very little. Then you will also not be honest with something very large.* Luke 16:10

Activity Options

☐ Read and discuss the prayer below, written by Alvin William "Smokey" Linn, a career firefighter from Wichita, Kansas. What words and phrases make you think of someone you can trust?

> *When I am called to duty, God, whenever flames may rage;*
> *Give me strength to save some life, whatever be its age.*
> *Help me embrace a little child before it is too late,*
> *Or save an older person from the horror of that fate.*
> *Enable me to be alert and hear the weakest shout,*
> *And quickly and efficiently to put the fire out.*
> *I want to fill my calling and to give the best in me,*
> *To guard my every neighbor and protect his property.*
> *And if, according to my fate, I am to lose my life;*
> *Please bless with your protecting hand my children and my wife.*

- People like Smokey Linn often teach about safety and first aid. Learn some basic first aid and steps of CPR (cardiopulmonary resuscitation). Check your family first aid kit and refill the supplies as needed.

- What can you do to be a person people trust? Share ideas to practice.

FAMILY DEVOTION
• READ ALOUD •

Fireman Smokey Linn 2 minutes

Steve looked at his dad and said, "Please tell the story of Firemen Smokey Linn."

Dad grinned, "As a teen, Alvin William Linn's grandpa kept a Model T truck in his barn. That was one of the first types of trucks ever made. Alvin saw flames coming from the barn, so he raced into the barn, jumped in the truck, and drove it out. As he came out, smoke puffed up out of his pants and that's how he got his name Smokey Linn."

Steve laughed and said, "Smokey Linn was always brave."

His dad nodded and said, "Smokey Linn served in the Coast Guard in WWII and is one of the few people to survive a torpedo attack. Then he became a firefighter whom people trusted. He was one of the first people to teach others CPR and first aid to help save lives."

Steve prompted, "But not every day was a happy day for Smokey Linn."

Dad nodded, "That's right. One day Smokey Linn saw the faces of three children in a window of a burning building and knew he and the other firefighters could not save them. He was devastated. He wrote a prayer that many firefighters say."

"Let's say the prayer together!" Steve said.

Bible Story Connection 3–4 minutes

Read Daniel 3, a story about three men who escaped a blazing, hot fire. Who helped them?

Chat Prompts

MORE TIME?

- *By day the LORD went ahead of them in a pillar of cloud. It guided them on their way. At night he led them with a pillar of fire. It gave them light. So they could travel by day or at night.* Exodus 13:21

  Chat about what you like about fires and discuss fire safety. How did God use fire to show his presence? What was special about the fire?

- *[Nehemiah] said to them, "You can see the trouble we're in. Jerusalem has been destroyed. Fire has burned up its gates. Come on. Let's rebuild the wall of Jerusalem. Then people won't be ashamed anymore."* Nehemiah 2:17

  Discuss the damage fires cause and the work to fix things. Chat about things you've helped repair.

- *The tongue is also a fire. The tongue is the most evil part of the body. It makes the whole body impure. It sets a person's whole way of life on fire.* James 3:6

  The Bible compares the tongue and words we say to fire. Talk about ways our words can be as destructive as a fire.

Scrapbook/Prayer Journal Options

Use art as a reminder of fire safety.

- Draw flames and write fire safety tips beside them.

- Draw a fire hat and remember to pray for firefighters.

- Draw something from your first aid kit and write a note on how to use it.

Frontline Tips

Develop a signal for family members to tell the rest of the family that they have had a tough day. Consider signals such as putting up a red flag or sitting a teddy bear on the kitchen counter. Encourage family members to notice the signal and give extra hugs and kind words to their struggling family member.

Prayer

Dear Lord, we thank you for the brave men and women who fight fires. Keep them safe. In Jesus' name, amen.

Wrap-Up

Talk about people who are willing to save people, even if it means they face danger.

Volunteer Attitudes

Family Beatitude: Happy is the family who serves with love for they will touch hearts.

Focus: Having a good attitude when serving

Weekly Bible Verse: *Serve your masters with all your heart. Work as serving the Lord and not as serving people.* Ephesians 6:7

Activity Options

☐ Find out if a neighbor or anyone from your church is having a hard time and might need help with doing home repairs or yard work, or with cooking meals. Plan to help out as a family.

☐ Consider going as a family to visit people in a nursing home to read or just sit and talk with patients.

☐ Practice serving one another at home: fetch things, serve snacks, let others have the first turn, and serve up lots of smiles and cheerful words.

FAMILY DEVOTION · READ ALOUD ·

Family Circle 2 minutes

Dad asked everyone to gather for devotions. The children gave him high-fives when they entered the room and saw a table filled with favorite flavors of ice cream and lots of toppings.

"Dad, are we talking about God's Word being sweet again?"

"No, I wanted to take time to thank all of you."

"What?" "Why?" "What did we do?" Questions whizzed at Dad from all directions.

Dad laughed and said, "You spent yesterday working hard to help other people. I know our house still needs lots of work from the hurricane damage, but most of what's left is for workmen to do. Girls, you went to a tent shelter for people who have no home left and played with the children, brought clothes, and helped people fill out forms. Sons, you went with me to work on someone's house. You learned how to put up drywall fast and did a lot in one day."

Bella said, "The children we watched were so sweet. I didn't realize how many reasons we have to give thanks. We still have a home. We still have most of our things. I wanted to cry for some of them because it was so sad. But instead, I smiled. And that cheered me up, too!"

James said, "Dad, I'm glad our scout leader is a contractor and that he taught us how to do home repairs. It felt good."

"I know none of you really wanted to get up so early, but you put on your smiles once you arrived and brought hope. You showed good servant attitudes. I'm thankful you are experiencing joy through serving others. So, let's dig in and then we'll share some verses about serving and attitudes."

Bible Story Connection 3–4 minutes

Read about four poor lepers who found treasure in an abandoned camp and shared the good news to help others, in 2 Kings 7:1–20. When have you shared the good news about a special deal with your friends and neighbors?

Chat Prompts

MORE TIME?

- *My brothers and sisters, you were chosen to be free. But don't use your freedom as an excuse to live under the power of sin. Instead, serve one another in love.* Galatians 5:13

   When have you given up free time for to help others? How did you make the choice? How do you feel about the time you gave up now?

- *Our God is a God who strengthens and encourages you. May he give you the same attitude toward one another that Christ Jesus had.* Romans 15:5

   What attitude did you see in Jesus when he served people (miracles, healings, washing feet)? What do you do when you have a negative attitude?

- *Jesus sat down and called for the 12 disciples to come to him. Then he said, "Anyone who wants to be first must be the very last. They must be the servant of everyone."* Mark 9:35

   How can you serve others? Do you always try to be first?

Scrapbook/Prayer Journal Options

Use art to remember God wants us to help others.

- Draw hammers, paintbrushes, and other tools used in helping to repair a home. Write about helping someone.

- Draw hearts with smiles and write about attitudes to have when serving others and tips on turning a negative attitude into a positive one.

- Draw a towel and feet and write about Jesus serving others.

Frontline Tips

- Be sure to pray together as a family before volunteering and check your attitudes before leaving home.

- Get a volunteer spirit going. Keep your eyes and ears open to notice if someone needs help.

Prayer

Dear Lord, you willingly served others. Thanks for opportunities for us to serve. Help us serve with our whole hearts. In Jesus' name, amen.

Wrap-Up

Discuss what you can do next to volunteer as a family.

92

Family Fitness

Family Beatitude: Happy is the family that walks and plays together, for they will be healthy.

Focus: Exercising for health

Weekly Bible Verse: *Those who trust in the LORD will receive new strength. They will fly as high as eagles. They will run and not get tired. They will walk and not grow weak.* Isaiah 40:31

Activity Options

☐ Make a commitment to try new ways to stay in shape as a family, like swimming, walking, playing ball, or indoor exercises. Take turns letting family members choose and lead exercises.

☐ Make plans to enter a family run and make sure you practice going the distance ahead of the race day.

☐ Organize a fitness day in your neighborhood.

☐ Add that spiritual element by taking prayer walks around your community and at local parks.

☐ Remember to have a positive attitude. Make smiley face buttons for everyone to wear.

Family Fun Run 2 minutes

"We won! We won!"

"Oh, Noble, did you and your brother reach the finish first in your age groups?"

"No, Mom. But they just called our family up to the award platform, so let's see what we won."

The Harper family stepped on the platform to receive a trophy.

The emcee announced, "Congratulations. You had the family with the most participants in our police fund raiser, our *Run-dezvous*. We even counted your little girl in the stroller since she crossed the finish line."

Mom read the engraved words, "Run-dezvous Family Award."

Everyone laughed and cheered. Their matching T-shirts made it easy for people to see the six Harpers. The emcee stuck a microphone out and asked Mr. Harper to speak.

Mr. Harper looked around and said, "Our family walks around the neighborhood to spend more time in the sun and less time with technology. We may not be fast, but we do play together and have fun. When I'm off duty I like to enjoy nature."

Mrs. Harper asked a friend to snap a photo with her cell phone.

That evening Mom said, "Let's add something new as we walk. Let's do a prayer walk."

Noble said, "We talked about that at church. We can pray for our neighbors and thank God for our home and friends as we walk."

Bible Story Connection 3–4 minutes

Read 1 Corinthians 9:24–27 and discuss running
races. Why do you need to focus on the goal?

Chat Prompts

MORE TIME?

- *Some men of Gad went over to David's side at his usual
  place of safety in the desert. They were brave fighting men.
  They were ready for battle. They were able to use shields and
  spears. Their faces were like the faces of lions. They could run
  as fast as antelopes in the mountains.* 1 Chronicles 12:8

  Chat about how firefighters, police officers, and
  military men and women need to be in good physical
  shape. What can you do to be physically fit?

- *Run away from the evil things that young people long
  for. Try hard to do what is right. Have faith, love and
  peace. Do these things together with those who call on
  the Lord from a pure heart.* 2 Timothy 2:22

  What should you run from? Why?

- *So obey God. Stand up to the devil. He will
  run away from you.* James 4:7

  How does it help you to obey God? How
  can you make the devil run?

Scrapbook/Prayer Journal Options

Share through art the joy of physical play with the family God gave you.

- Draw sneakers and write about running.
- Draw a trophy and write ways your family is a winning family.
- Draw a running path and write on it words about obeying God or write prayers for neighbors.

Frontline Tips

- Find a local trail or hiking area your family enjoys and plan times to hike and picnic.
- It's harder for men and women at sea or in planes most of the day to get exercise. Sitting at a desk all day is also hard. Share ways to stretch and move even in smaller spaces.

Prayer

Dear Lord, help our family stay fit and have fun together. In Jesus' name, amen.

Wrap-Up

Chat about the ways you play and stay healthy as a family.

Wildfires, Smoke, & Safety

Family Beatitude: Happy is the family who trusts God, for they know real security.

Focus: Fostering real security

Weekly Bible Verse: *They put out great fires. They escaped being killed by swords. Their weakness was turned to strength. They became powerful in battle. They beat back armies from other countries.* Hebrews 11:34

Activity Options

☐ Discuss emergency plans and possible natural disasters that could happen where you live.

☐ Check your fire extinguisher and talk about how to use it. Talk about what is best to use to put out different types of fires.

☐ Think of an area that has been damaged by a disaster and do something to help the people there, such as sending a gift card for hardware supplies to a church in that area or a disaster-relief organization. Or, send cookies to the fire departments or other workers who helped in the disaster area.

Evacuation 2 minutes

Raquel shook her sleeping daughter. "Christy, wake up. We have leave. There's a big wildfire a few towns away and our house may not be here when we come back."

"My toys! I need my dino toy." Christy ran and picked up her dino and a few other toys.

Raquel said, "Great! And I have others in the car already. Let's take your blanket, too."

"Where's Daddy?"

"Because he's a firefighter, he's already left. He needs to help put out the fire. Let's pray for him and the other firefighters to be safe."

"God, keep my daddy safe and help him not let our house burn down."

Raquel loaded her infant son and Christy in the car that she had packed as full as possible. She drove off at two o'clock in the morning. Thankfully they always kept the car fueled. The gas stations were packed with people trying to fill their tanks.

The roads were also filled with cars making it difficult to get anywhere. When they finally reached a safe town, they pulled into a parking lot and waited for hours. Cell towers had burned down. Raquel waited anxiously for a text from her husband, Adam. At last, he texted that he remained safe.

When authorities said it was safe to do so, they returned home. They all hugged when Adam arrived home. That was when Raquel noticed the scorching on his pants.

Later that night Adam explained the chaos the firefighters had faced. Unlike serving on strike teams in other towns, he was on duty when more calls came in than they could manage. When he took a turn fighting the fires, he came so close that the flames seemed to lick him. They focused on saving lives and evacuating people, even taking some people in the fire trucks. Homes of friends burned to the ground, but somehow their house survived.

Bible Story Connection 3–4 minutes

Read Numbers 11:1–3 about a time God sent a blazing fire that burned edges of a camp and how he stopped it when the people cried for help.

Chat Prompts

- *I keep my eyes always on the LORD. He is at my right hand. So I will always be secure.* Psalm 16:8

  How can you keep your eyes on God, especially when you are afraid?

- *The tongue is a small part of a person's body. But it talks big. Think about how a small spark can set a big forest on fire.* James 3:5

  Talk about how words can hurt and burn our hearts. Say something nice to each family member. Practice thinking before you speak.

- *The LORD your God is like a fire that burns everything up. He wants you to worship only him.* Deuteronomy 4:24

  Chat about God being like a fire and how we are to worship him, the one true God.

Scrapbook/Prayer Journal Options

Use art as a reminder that God cares about our troubles, too.

- Draw your car and write notes of what you would take in an emergency evacuation.
- Draw eyes and write about looking to God when troubles come.
- Draw a tongue and write about ways to control your words.

Frontline Tips

Arrange to have an emergency contact who lives in a different area. Make sure everyone in your family knows that you can all call that person during emergencies if you are not able to reach one another. This is especially important if anyone is a first responder and duty keeps them on the scene of the emergency. Make sure everyone memorizes the contact information for the emergency contact.

Prayer

Lord, we look to you and trust that you know our future. Keep us safe and calm. In Jesus' name, amen.

Wrap-Up

Share tips to remember in an emergency.

Joy of Shared Meals

Family Beatitude: Happy is the family who eats together, for they will be nurtured.

Focus: Eating together

Weekly Bible Verse: *Make the most of every opportunity. The days are evil.* Ephesians 5:16

Activity Options

☐ Let each person have time to talk at meals. Draw the quiet ones out by chatting about their favorite activities. Turn off technology for family time (except for a family member on call).

☐ Plan a silly together time after sharing a meal, like a foam-ball fight, painting funny faces on each other, or making crazy ice cream sundaes.

☐ Make simple bread sticks: Mix equal amounts of self-rising flour and yogurt. Pull off balls of the dough and roll into snake-like tubes. Brush with olive oil and sprinkle on a favorite flavoring (minced garlic, oregano, cheese, etc.). Bake at 425°F for five to ten minutes. Turn halfway through cooking. Alternatively, cook in air fryer at 400°F for four to eight minutes.

Big Family Breakfast **2 minutes**

Riley woke her daughter, Kiona, and her son, Gary, up early, "It's the day of our big family breakfast!"

The children jumped up and Gary shouted, "Hooray! We're all together!"

With their busy schedules, Allen's changing hours as a policeman, and Riley's part-time job, it was hard to have family time. They started a tradition of a big breakfast once a week at home or a favorite restaurant. When Allen got off his night shift and wasn't on call, they surprised the children with an early morning meal.

Allen spread syrup on his pancakes to make a funny face. Kiona used strawberries to make a flower. They laughed and shared what had happened in the past few days.

Gary asked, "Dad, did you have to catch bad people?"

"My partner and I stopped someone from stealing, but most of the time it was quiet in the town. People obeyed the laws."

Kiona said, "I wish everyone would be good."

Allen smiled, "I'm happy you are good and obey us. I heard you got a star on your spelling test."

"You helped me study. You're a good dad." Kiona said.

Riley said, "I'm thankful we have a good family. What's everyone thankful for today?"

Each one gave one or two examples of what they felt thankful for. Talking about blessings is how they always ended the big family breakfast.

Bible Story Connection 3–4 minutes

Read John 21:1–14 about a time Jesus had breakfast
with his disciples after they had not seen him in a while.
Talk about the fun of picnics and eating together.

Chat Prompts

- *Go and enjoy your food. Be joyful as you drink your wine.
  God has already approved what you do.* Ecclesiastes 9:7

  Talk about enjoying time together and understanding
  that God approves when we make good choices.

- *There is a time for everything. There's a time for
  everything that is done on earth.* Ecclesiastes 3:1

  Chat about when your family spends time together and
  what plans you want to make for fun together. Talk about
  the times family members need to work or volunteer.

- *Those who do right can expect joy. But the hopes of
  sinners are bound to fail.* Proverbs 10:28

  Chat about the joy of making good choices and
  having things go well. Discuss what *joy* means.

Scrapbook/Prayer Journal Options

Create an art memory of your family mealtimes.

- Draw a table or plate and write about times you eat together as a family.

- Draw a star and write about stars you get for doing good things.

- Draw smiles and write what makes each person thankful.

Frontline Tips

- Create some family traditions that help you celebrate being together. Snap photos at these times.

- For families with extended time apart, schedule an online party or prerecord messages to play when the rest of the family is together. Ahead of time, mail party favors to the absent family member so that they can feel a part of the celebration.

Prayer

Father, we thank you for times our family can eat together and have fun together. In Jesus' name, amen.

Wrap-Up

Let each person share a favorite memory of family meals.

104

Disaster Response

Family Beatitude: Happy is the family who responds to the needs of friends, for they will be appreciated.

Focus: Volunteering to help after disasters

Weekly Bible Verse: *Don't forget to do good. Don't forget to share with others. God is pleased with those kinds of offerings.* Hebrews 13:16

Activity Options

☐ As a family, set aside time to go through your pantry and closets to find items to give to the needy. Ask each family member to think of one treasured item they can give away.

☐ Help out at a fundraiser or find a way to help raise money for disaster relief.

☐ Think of friends, neighbors, or people you read about who struggle from a disaster, illness, or joblessness. Choose one thing to do for them, such as not having dessert for a week and using the money to buy a gas gift card for them.

Disaster Support 2 minutes

Leah prepared to help with another pancake breakfast while her husband, Walt, donned his work boots. He gave her a quick kiss before leaving to sift through ashes where their friends' homes had stood.

While she worked at the pancake breakfast, Leah's mom kept an eye on her young son. Her daughter, Erica, helped by putting out napkins and clearing away plates after people finished eating.

The wildfires had devoured the homes of other firefighters while their home remained intact. The brotherhood of firefighters remained tight and lent support to one another. The weekly pancake breakfast and other efforts to raise funds had kept those who lost their homes hopeful. They also served to meet some of their needs in the process of waiting on insurance and rebuilding. Other volunteers helped by finding items that survived the flames, like metal boxes that held important papers and tools.

Driving past the charred lots helped the children understand the seriousness of it all. Erica had chosen some of her favorite toys and gave them to her friend Jill who had lost almost all of her toys. Jill also had a weekly play date at Erica's house. Erica let her friends borrow games, dolls, and stuffed animals. They switched them out each week.

Walt praised his daughter and said, "Erica you are such a great help to our friends. They are so thankful that you are sharing your favorite toys."

Erica said, "It will be fun when Jill has her new home and all new toys. Look! She lent me her new game and taught me how to play it. She's helpful, too, even if she lost her house."

Bible Story Connection 3–4 minutes

Read Matthew 25:35–40 to discover ways Jesus said we could help others. Discuss which of these ways you can help.

Chat Prompts

MORE TIME?

- *The earth may fall apart. The mountains may fall into the middle of the sea. But we will not be afraid.* Psalm 46:2

    Why don't we need to be afraid of disasters? How can you always be pray-pared?

- *God's gifts of grace come in many forms. Each of you has received a gift in order to serve others. You should use it faithfully.* 1 Peter 4:10

    Talk about your talents and how you can use them to help others.

- *They help one another. They say to one another, "Be strong!"* Isaiah 41:6

    Chat about ways to encourage others with kind words that bring hope.

Scrapbook/Prayer Journal Options

Use art to share how your family uses talents to help others.

- Draw a picture of a fire or flood and write about how a disaster causes damage.

- Trace your hand and write ways to serve people.

- Draw a gift box. Write on it some of your talents that are gifts and how you use them to help others.

Frontline Tips

- As a family called to serve, find ways to help other families who also serve but are now in need.

- When you have difficulties, forget your pride and share your struggle with another family who serves. You'll find strong bonds within your field of service.

Prayer

Dear Father, help us look to the needs of others and be willing to share the blessings you have given us. In Jesus' name, amen.

Wrap-Up

Discuss one thing to do that will help a family in need.

Our Unique Family

Family Beatitude: Happy is the family who prays for people in need, for they will be a blessing.

Focus: Seeing life differently

Weekly Bible Verse: *No one should look out for their own interests. Instead, they should look out for the interests of others.* 1 Corinthians 10:24

Activity Options

☐ Pray when you hear a siren or news of a disaster. Pray for the people involved as well as the rescue workers and medical personnel.

☐ Staying strong and healthy enables us to help others. Exercise and eat well. Try building muscles by pumping water bottles. Lift the bottles up and down. Drink water, too, because water energizes your muscles. As the bottles empty, the exercise will get easier!

☐ When an alarm or siren goes off, look, listen, and follow directions.

Siren Prayers **2 minutes**

Kitty said, "Mom, I hear a siren. God wants us to pray."

Alice pulled over and stopped the car. They started to pray for the people who might be hurt and the people caring for them.

Kitty looked out the window and said, "Why didn't other cars stop to pray?"

"God calls people to do different things. Your dad rescues people, so we always notice the sirens and flashing lights. That makes us think about emergencies and people in need."

"I'm so happy that Daddy likes to save people."

"Yes. He cares about others. We care about his safety and the safety of people who drive ambulances, fire trucks, police cars, and all those who care for people in emergencies."

Alice heard more sirens and knew that meant a larger emergency. Her husband was on ambulance duty and might come home very tired and feeling discouraged. She said, "Remember when we hear sirens and Daddy is on duty that he might be tired when he comes home."

"We could bake his favorite cookies. That makes him smile. I pray for Daddy every night, so he will be strong and healthy."

"That's great. We'll make cookies when we get home."

Bible Story Connection 3–4 minutes

Read James 5:13–15 about praying for the sick. Chat about praying when you see an ambulance or fire truck with lights flashing.

Chat Prompts

- *God has saved us from deadly dangers. And he will continue to do it. We have put our hope in him. He will continue to save us. You must help us by praying for us. Then many people will give thanks because of what will happen to us. They will thank God for his kindness to us in answer to the prayers of many.* 2 Corinthians 1:10–11

   Discuss how prayers help people. How do you pray for one another in your family and how does that help? How can answers to prayers cause other people to praise God?

- *Wise people see danger and go to a safe place. But childish people keep going and suffer for it.* Proverbs 22:3

   Discuss what makes you know there's an emergency and how you should react.

- *Finally, I want all of you to agree with one another. Be understanding. Love one another. Be kind and tender. Be humble.* 1 Peter 3:8

   Talk about praying for people you don't know, like someone hurt in an accident or fire. What does it mean to be tender or sympathetic?

Scrapbook/Prayer Journal Options

Show that your family is loving and caring like God wants you to be.

- Draw a siren and write about praying for people who are hurt and those who help them.

- Draw a bandage and write about how your family cares for one another when someone is sick or hurt.

- Draw a sad face and a happy face and write about what makes someone sad and what cheers someone up.

Frontline Tips

Make a peaceful spot in your home where a weary worker or volunteer can relax and recover from a tough day.

Prayer

Dear Lord, help us be attentive to the needs of others and keep first responders strong and safe. In Jesus' name, amen.

Wrap-Up

Talk about sirens and why emergency vehicles use them.

Moving Adventures

> **Family Beatitude:** Happy is the family who finds adventure in moving for they will make more friends.
>
> **Focus:** Finding adventure in moving
>
> **Weekly Bible Verse:** *From a place far away I call out to you. I call out as my heart gets weaker. Lead me to the safety of a rock that is high above me.* Psalm 61:2

Activity Options

- [ ] Make some friend cards. Print out cards with your name and parent-approved phone or other contact information. Add a few of your favorite interests. These are good to pass out when you have moved or meet someone who recently moved to your area.

- [ ] Plan a get-together at a park or your home and invite friends. Try to invite at least one new person who might need a friend.

- [ ] Stay connected when you or a friend move. Set up times to chat by phone, video, or online.

FAMILY DEVOTION · READ ALOUD ·

Finding Our New Home 2 minutes

The family gathered together. Jon said, "It's that time. We are moving to Oklahoma. I know we have enjoyed Florida and made great friends. We'll come back to vacation here."

Karli and Jon fielded questions from their children. Then they set everything in motion from packing up every room to driving across country with three vehicles. Three months later they settled in the new home and started making friends. Jordan enjoyed her girl's running club where they talked about healthy living and she easily made friends.

One day Russ sat in the kitchen playing with his snack. Karli asked him, "How are you feeling?"

"I miss my friends. It's been hard. But I'm glad you have a job you like, Mom."

"Thanks, Russ. I miss my Florida friends, too. In an hour you will be online chatting with your pal. It must be hard for you to live in this rural area after being in a development with so many kids your age."

"I'm trying to do what Dad said and bloom where we are being planted. I think I'm slow at sprouting and growing here. At least I have friends at church."

"Your brother, Jackson, is happy you have more time for him."

"He's starting to be more fun. He likes to play cars and build things with me." He paused for a moment. "Mom? I think I need a hug."

They moved to sit on the couch, hugged, and talked about the friends they missed as well as made plans to get together with new friends."

Bible Story Connection 3–4 minutes

Read Genesis 12:1–5 and discuss how Abram and his family moved to an unknown area when God asked him to move.

Chat Prompts

- *"I know the plans I have for you," announces the* LORD. *"I want you to enjoy success. I do not plan to harm you. I will give you hope for the years to come."* Jeremiah 29:11

  Discuss how we need to trust God with our future and where we live. How has he helped you make friends?

MORE TIME?

- *The* LORD *himself will go ahead of you. He will be with you. He will never leave you. He'll never desert you. So don't be afraid. Don't lose hope.* Deuteronomy 31:8

  Chat about how God prepares the way when you move and how he is always with you.

- *By wisdom a house is built. Through understanding it is made secure.* Proverbs 24:3

  Discuss how understanding is important, especially when we experience changes.

Scrapbook/Prayer Journal Options

Use art to share about your neighborhood or feelings.

- Draw a house and write about your home and neighborhood.

- Draw a moving truck and write about you or someone you know who moved.

- Draw an ear and write about how it helps to have someone listen to your feelings.

Frontline Tips

- Chat about how pioneers circled the wagons for protection and how that helped them rely on one another. Discuss ways to rely on your family members, especially when you move.

- Start a list of ways to make new friends and activities to do as a family when you live in a new area and don't have friends yet (like exploring parks and places in the area and joining church activities).

Prayer

Dear Father, help us trust you when we have to do something hard, like moving. Be with us wherever we live. In Jesus' name, amen.

Wrap-Up

Chat about what it's like to move someplace new.

Freedom of Speech

Family Beatitude: Happy is the family who values freedom of speech for they will share ideas.

Focus: Speaking with freedom

Weekly Bible Verse: *You will know the truth. And the truth will set you free.* John 8:32

Activity Options

☐ Wear a cross or other symbols of your faith and be ready to reply if someone comments or asks questions about your faith. Find Open Doors U.S.A. online and check out its list of countries where it's hard to be a Christian.

☐ Hang your flag outside, gather around it, and pray to thank God for freedom of religion and speech in America.

☐ Be happy you can share your faith. Invite a friend to your church or a church event.

Ministry in Nepal 2 minutes

Sandra and her family lived in Nepal and ran a small business. They wanted to share the gospel, but as Americans they knew they had to follow Nepal's governmental rules. No one in that country is allowed to change their religion. They must remain in the faith of their parents.

Sandra and her brothers and sisters knew they had to be careful with words and show their faith by actions of love. They met people and once they became friends they could answer questions people asked. Neighbors always watched and asked questions.

On the Fourth of July they decorated their door in red, white, and blue and wore those colors. When friends asked about the door, they explained about the holiday back in the United States and how they valued their freedom of speech and freedom of religion. They answered similar questions about their Christmas and Easter decorations. Those days gave them opportunities to share their faith.

In the evenings, Sandra and her family prayed, read the Bible, and shared about their conversations with people. Sandra said, "It's hard to keep so much inside me. I want to tell people what Jesus has done for me."

Her father said, "Many people here believe in other gods and fear that we make those gods mad. We live our faith and pray for God to open their minds and hearts."

Bible Story Connection 3–4 minutes

Read Acts 16:16–31 about how people beat Paul for his beliefs. They threw him in prison, but God set him free and used the incident to convert the jailer.

Chat Prompts

- *Blessed are you when people make fun of you and hurt you because of me. You are also blessed when they tell all kinds of evil lies about you because of me.* Matthew 5:11

  Talk about being bullied or teased for your faith and how to stand firm.

- *Even the Son of Man did not come to be served. Instead, he came to serve others. He came to give his life as the price for setting many people free.* Mark 10:45

  How does knowing Jesus served others help you think of ways you can help others?

- *Live as free people. But don't use your freedom to cover up evil. Live as people who are God's slaves.* 1 Peter 2:16

  How does freedom give you choices to do good or evil? How can you live for God and be a servant to God?

Scrapbook/Prayer Journal Options

Use art to show you are thankful for freedom.

- Draw a flag and write about freedom.
- Draw a mouth and write a prayer for missionaries.
- Draw a cross or fish and write about symbols that show your faith.

Frontline Tips

- Before traveling to a foreign country, study the customs and find out about their religious freedom.
- If you live where it is against the law to share your faith, do prayer walks and wear a fish pin or other Christian symbol that may be less known than a cross.

Prayer

Dear Father, help missionaries as they serve around the world and let them be free to speak about Jesus. In Jesus' name, amen.

Wrap-Up

Discuss the many blessings of freedom.

Making a Difference

Family Beatitude: Happy is the family who strives to make a difference, for they will be influencers.

Focus: Making a difference in people's lives

Weekly Bible Verse: *Suppose one of you has 100 sheep and loses one of them. Won't he leave the 99 in the open country? Won't he go and look for the one lost sheep until he finds it? When he finds it, he will joyfully put it on his shoulders.* Luke 15:4–5

Activity Options

☐ The Civil Air Patrol is an organization for high school students interested in serving in the Air Force. Check out organizations that help people. Talk about ways you can help people and groups you might want to join that assist in your community.

☐ Discuss what to do if you get lost. Talk about standing "still and tall" to be found. Or discuss where to go, such as the first checkout counter in a store or the place you last saw your parent.

☐ Discuss how groups perform search-and-rescue missions.

Night Patrol 2 minutes

"Josh, your phone is ringing!" Mom called from the kitchen. Josh appeared with shaving cream on one side of his face and a razor in hand. He picked up the phone and listened. "Yep, I'm on my way." He washed his face, slipped into his uniform and grabbed his backpack.

That evening at dinner Josh shared what happened.

"My Civil Air Patrol (CAP) unit got a call to help find a lost child. I was still a little sleepy and raced to get there. Suddenly, a police siren came up behind me. I pulled over and took my license out of my wallet. The cop looked at my uniform and said, 'Follow me.' We sped all the way to our base location."

Josh went on to tell how he then signed in and his leader sent him with a buddy to search a specific area. They used their flashlights and checked behind every tree and boulder. They walked quietly listening for sounds like crying and carefully watched where they stepped in case the child had fallen.

An hour or so after Josh arrived, they heard the signal to return to base. One pair of CAP cadets located the missing child and the search ended. Josh watched the parents hug their young son.

His family congratulated him for being part of a successful mission.

Bible Story Connection 3–4 minutes

Read Luke 15:1–6 about finding a lost sheep and how much you care for your family members.

Chat Prompts

MORE TIME?

- *Like a lost sheep, I've gone down the wrong path. Come and look for me, because I haven't forgotten to obey your commands.* Psalm 119:176

  Talk about a different kind of "lost" that is being separated from God. Chat about how forgiveness restores us and brings us back to God.

- *I will search for the lost. I will bring back those who have wandered away. I will bandage the ones who are hurt. I will make the weak ones stronger. But I will destroy those who are fat and strong. I will take good care of my sheep. I will treat them fairly.* Ezekiel 34:16

  These words show commitment and dedication to helping others. It's a promise. Discuss what you can promise to do to help others, like treating people fairly, using kind words, opening doors, or tithing your money.

- *The LORD will command his angels to take good care of you.* Psalm 91:11

  Chat about trusting God if you are ever lost or need help.

Scrapbook/Prayer Journal Options

- With art or journaling, share your family safety rules.

- Draw a flashlight and write about staying with your family when you go places.

- Draw a compass and write about following directions.

- Draw a lamb and write about the story of the lost lamb.

Frontline Tips

If there is a family member who is often called to serve without warning, have them share what is in their work bag. What do they take with them at a moment's notice?

Prayer

Dear Father, show us how we can help others this week. In Jesus' name, amen.

Wrap-Up

Discuss ways to help others. How can helping others show your faith in God?

Serving Together

> **Family Beatitude:** Happy is the family who serves together, for they will live in harmony.
>
> **Focus:** Investing in family volunteering and cooperation
>
> **Weekly Bible Verse:** *One person could be overpowered. But two people can stand up for themselves. And a rope made out of three cords isn't easily broken.* Ecclesiastes 4:12

Activity Options

☐ Give each family member one dollar and ask how they could each use it for their family. Then chat about putting the money together and what you could do as a family.

☐ Hold a tug-of-war and then play jump rope. Discuss how it's hard pulling against each other and fun when you can cooperate in play.

☐ When you go to social events or volunteer together consider wearing matching colors or even buy or make matching T-shirts.

Serving Together 2 minutes

Russ walked around the tables passing out extra rolls and talking to the people. His family served meals for the homeless every week and Josh enjoyed helping. At age nine, Russ had moved a few times because his dad served in the army. He felt a bit homeless when they left one home until they settled into the next and understood the people he served.

Russ and his family also collected clothes, hygiene items, bicycles, tents, and sleeping bags for the homeless. Russ liked watching his dad repair broken bicycles and handing him the tools he needed. They handed the items out after providing meals. They often served two hundred people including quite a few children. Then everyone who wanted to attend went into the church for service. He remembered when everyone fit at two tables. Now they filled the room.

Serving together helped Russ understand why his dad served people in the army. When his dad traveled, Russ felt less lonely since he had lots of homeless friends.

One day, as Russ passed out rolls, his dad came in. Russ yelled, "Dad, you're home! I thought you were off on orders."

His dad came over and they gave each other a high-five. Dad said, "I got back early. I knew I'd find you and the rest of the family serving people here. You're doing a great job in serving people. I like helping here because we do it together."

Bible Story Connection 3–4 minutes

Read Acts 2:42–47 and talk about togetherness and
what early church believers did together.

Chat Prompts

MORE TIME?

- *How good and pleasant it is when God's people
live together in peace!* Psalm 133:1

    Chat about harmony in your family and
    what makes it easier to live together.

- *You Gentiles, be full of joy. Be joyful together
with God's people.* Romans 15:10

    Discuss being joyful with one another, as well
    as with friends and your church family. Think
    of ways to sprinkle joy into people's lives.

- *Then I will come to you with joy just as God has planned.
We will be renewed by being together.* Romans 15:32

    Discuss the joy of being together as a family, especially
    if one parent was away for work for a while. How does
    serving together make your family stronger or happier?

Scrapbook/Prayer Journal Options

Share with art or words how your family serves people.

- Draw bread and write about serving together.

- Draw a suitcase and write about times your family has someone away for work or a trip.

- Add musical notes to your journal and write about what brings harmony in your family.

Frontline Tips

- Make the most of being together by planning special family activities, especially for any homecoming times.

- Check with your church and community to find ways to serve together.

Prayer

Dear Father, thanks for blessing us with talents we can share in serving others. In Jesus' name, amen.

Wrap-Up

Chat about what it means to each of you to serve others.

Safety Rules

Family Beatitude: Happy is the family who teaches safety, for they will be responsible.

Focus: Teaching safety with tools and weapons

Weekly Bible Verse: *Next to Binnui, Ezer repaired another part of the wall. He was the son of Jeshua. Ezer ruled over Mizpah. He repaired the part across from the place that went up to the storeroom where the weapons were kept. He repaired the wall up to the angle of the wall.* Nehemiah 3:19

Activity Options

☐ Talk about safety with weapons, tools, and knives. Practice safely by using a plastic knife. Make a cardboard jackknife with a paper fastener to hold the parts together for more knife safety practice.

☐ Practice safety at home by inspecting things like electrical outlets and plugs.

☐ Practice safely walking on streets without sidewalks and crossing streets. Plan an escape route from your home in case of danger.

Daddy, Can I Touch Your Gun? 2 minutes

Lars raced to the door as his dad entered. He reached up and touched the holster and gun.

His father moved Lars's hand away and said, "You cannot touch my gun."

Lars stepped back and stared at his daddy.

His father asked, "Do you want to see my gun?" Lars nodded.

Douglas pulled out the gun and held it with his hand covering the trigger. He let Lars look, and then asked, "Do you want to touch the gun?" Lars nodded.

Douglas showed him where he could touch it. Then he talked about the danger of guns and other weapons. He said, "I had a lot of training with guns and safety. I need this to protect good people, but it is not a toy. It can hurt people."

Lars said, "Mommy says that guns are not toys. That's why she doesn't want us to have toy guns. You're a police officer, so you need a gun."

Douglas said, "That's right." He tousled Lars's hair, locked up his holster and gun, and said, "Let me put away my gun and then we can get some toys and play together."

Bible Story Connection 3–4 minutes

Read 1 Samuel 20:19–24, 32–42 that tells how Jonathon protected
David to keep him safe. How did Jonathan use his arrows?

Chat Prompts

- *He will judge between the nations. He'll settle problems
  among many of them. They will hammer their swords
  into plows. They'll hammer their spears into pruning
  tools. Nations will not go to war against one another.
  They won't even train to fight anymore.* Isaiah 2:4

    Talk about peace and how one day God
    will bring peace to the world.

- *Our fight is not against human beings. It is against the rulers,
  the authorities and the powers of this dark world. It is against the
  spiritual forces of evil in the heavenly world.* Ephesians 6:12

    Discuss spiritual battles. Look up the armor of God in
    Ephesians 6:10–17. How can God's Word be a weapon?

- *In peace I will lie down and sleep. LORD,
  you alone keep me safe.* Psalm 4:8

    What can you do to have peace in your home and with
    your friends? What helps you fall asleep without fear?

Scrapbook/Prayer Journal Options

Write or draw about peace.

- Draw a dove and write about it being a symbol of peace.

- Draw sad faces and write about how people use weapons to hurt people.

- Draw a bed with someone sleeping and write how God gives us peace.

Frontline Tips

- For workers who need weapons, discuss the importance of safety with weapons.

- Be sure your children know why you lock weapons in a safe and secure place.

Prayer

Father, protect us from harm and help the men and women who work to keep people safe. In Jesus' name, amen.

Wrap-Up

Chat about safety in your home.

Bridging the Distance

Family Beatitude: Happy is the family who communicates well for they will stay connected.

Focus: Staying connected

Weekly Bible Verse: *[Love] always protects. It always trusts. It always hopes. It never gives up.* 1 Corinthians 13:7

Activity Options

☐ People like to feel like they belong in the family. Be sure to pass out lots of hugs and encouraging words to one another.

☐ Use honey on toast or apple slices. Talk about how sweet it is and how sweet words keep us closer. We don't want bad things like dirt in our mouth, nor should we let bad words go out of our mouths.

☐ Make a board of encouraging words to say and see how much you can use them this week.

Daddy's Online 2 minutes

Mom called out, "Daddy's online!"

Ethan and Lily ran to the computer and said, "Hi, Daddy!"

Their father, Michael, said, "Hi, kids." He held up a cupcake. "Happy birthday, Ethan!"

Ethan grinned, "I'm having a party with my friends later."

Michael said, "I know. I'll be watching from the computer to celebrate your special day with you! After you blow out the candles on your cake, I'll eat my cupcake while you eat your cake. I left a present there for you to open. I love you."

"I love you, too, Daddy."

Grandma walked in with some wrapped gifts. She said, "Before your friends get here, let's open the presents from your dad. Lily, there's one for you, too!" Grandma handed each child a wrapped package.

Ethan unwrapped a small remote-controlled helicopter and Lily opened up a bell decorated with a fairy. She rang the bell while Grandma and Ethan sent the helicopter soaring.

As Ethan's friends showed up, they saw Ethan's dad on the screen and greeted him. Michael stayed online as long as he could, watching the party and listening. Ethan's mom took photos and messaged them to Ethan's dad.

That night Ethan said, "I'm glad Daddy came to my party and talked to me."

Bible Story Connection 3–4 minutes

Read 2 Timothy 1:1–4. Paul loved Timothy like a son and missed him when they were apart. Talk about missing one another when you cannot be together.

Chat Prompts

- *Kind words are like honey. They are sweet to the spirit and bring healing to the body.* Proverbs 16:24

    This is more wisdom from Proverbs. Talk about what words you will remember while apart and how kind words help you.

MORE TIME?

- *Don't let any evil talk come out of your mouths. Say only what will help to build others up and meet their needs. Then what you say will help those who listen.* Ephesians 4:29

    These words remind us to be honest, not get angry, and to be kind and forgiving. Let each person have time to express love. Positive words help us feel connected. Talk about not being angry that a parent is deployed.

- *The right ruling at the right time is like golden apples in silver jewelry.* Proverbs 25:11

    Talk about how a pretty apple looks delicious. Chat about how you remember words people have said to you. Encouraging words or words of praise are great to remember and think about.

Scrapbook/Prayer Journal Options

Add art to express thoughts and words to remember while apart.

- Draw lips and add word bubbles with encouraging words.

- Add a candy kiss or hug with sweet words.

- Draw a ribbon for family ties. Write ways you plan to stay connected.

Frontline Tips

- Let the absent family member record a message on a cell phone or other device before leaving. At bedtime, play the message for children. Record online conversations to play back.

- If possible, schedule a time to connect online or face talk by cell phone.

- Make a paper chain of days of the deployment. Ask the family member deploying to write secret messages inside some of the links.

Prayer

Lord, help us to say the words each person needs to keep in their heart while we are apart. Help us use kind words and remember to be loyal to every member of our family. In Jesus' name, amen.

Wrap-Up

Talk about what activities help you while one parent is absent.

Responsibility

Family Beatitude: Happy is the family who accepts responsibilities, for they will be confident.

Focus: Fostering dependability

Weekly Bible Verse: *"Why were you looking for me?" [Jesus] asked. "Didn't you know I had to be in my Father's house?"* Luke 2:49

Activity Options

☐ Make a chore chart of what is reasonable for each person to do. Change it as little ones master a skill and are ready for new challenges.

☐ Have a reward system for doing chores regularly for a week or month.

☐ Discuss and examine excuses. For most of the week, whenever someone makes an excuse or tries to blame someone else for something, write down the words they say. At the end of the week, hold a family meeting and discuss each one. What was valid and what was really irresponsibility?

The Man of the House 2 minutes

The families of the crew had gathered for a meal after the ship deployed. Some of the fathers had reminded their sons to be helpful and be the man of the home while they were away. Many took that seriously.

One of the older boys pointed to a toddler. "Look at Marco. He's not even two, but while his dad's away, he's the man of the house now!"

The next morning, Marco's mom spotted him in the bathroom with shaving cream on and a razor in his hand. She grabbed the razor and said. "Marco, this will cut you and you'll bleed. Let me get one that's just right for you."

They shopped that day and picked up a toy razor that was blue, his favorite color. She also took him shopping for shoes, but he refused to try on sneakers. He kept picking up a pair of black shoes. Finally, she realized he wanted to wear shoes like his dad's uniform shoes. They bought the black ones—plus the sneakers.

At home, Marco's mom explained, "Being like daddy and the man of the house isn't just about shaving or dressing like a grown man. It really means helping out more. You could help me pick things up and fold laundry like daddy does when he's home."

Marco helped, and his mom said, "Great job, Marco. Daddy will be so proud that you are helping me and doing some things he usually does for us. You are being responsible."

Marco grinned and then raced off to play wearing his black shoes.

Bible Story Connection 3–4 minutes

Read 1 Samuel 3 about Samuel who served in the temple as a young boy and heard God speak to him. He helped God the Father. Talk about ways to help our heavenly father.

Chat Prompts

MORE TIME?

- *Then [Jesus] went back to Nazareth with [Mary and Joseph], and he obeyed them. But his mother kept all these things like a secret treasure in her heart.* Luke 2:51

  Chat about how Jesus wanted to start his work at a young age. What did he do? Why is it good to start earning a little money at a young age or start doing chores?

- *His master replied, "You have done well, good and faithful slave! You have been faithful with a few things. I will put you in charge of many things. Come and share your master's happiness!"* Matthew 25:21

  This is from the parable of the talents in Matthew 25:14–30. These words praised the person who worked hard to increase the money from his boss. Discuss what *responsibility* means.

  What talents and abilities does each person have to help the family? Who is doing that? How does it help your family?

- *In the same way, let your light shine so others can see it. Then they will see the good things you do. And they will bring glory to your Father who is in heaven.* Matthew 5:16

  Chat about how helping out together sets a good example for others. How can that also show your faith? How does it help for other people to see your family following God and loving one another?

Scrapbook/Prayer Journal Options

Add art to show how your family is responsible.

- Add stars with the names of family members who have been faithful to do their chores.

- Trace a hand. Write on the hand about skills people learn from doing chores.

- Add a candle with a glowing light as a reminder that your good work is noticed and brings glory to God.

Frontline Tips

Make a list of chores that an absent family member usually does but obviously can't do while away. Let children volunteer to take on some of those tasks. Be sure to thank them for the extra work.

Prayer

Father, thank you for giving us strong arms and legs so we can be helpful. Help us be responsible and to be lights that show your love. In Jesus' name, amen.

Wrap-Up

Discuss what you learned about responsibility and how many skills you've learn through doing chores.

Thoughtfulness

Family Beatitude: Happy is the family who sees a need and fills it, for they will be considered thoughtful.

Focus: Noticing and fulfilling needs

Weekly Bible Verse: *Don't do anything only to get ahead. Don't do it because you are proud. Instead, be humble. Value others more than yourselves.* Philippians 2:3

Activity Options

☐ Play a version of I Spy—I Spy a Need. See who can notice when a family member might like a little help, or a friend might need help. After identifying a need, figure out a way to address that need and serve the person. Share your successes with the whole family.

☐ Keep bottles of water handy to offer outside workers you see on your way to work, on your drive home, or on your street.

☐ Make some cookies and freeze some of the dough to slice and bake when you identify someone who could use a treat. Or keep meal ingredients on hand to provide a meal for a family in need.

Posted Need Online 2 minutes

"Look at this." Bianca shared news she read during her break. A local boy named Camden got dizzy at school and medical tests later showed his heart was plumbed backwards.

That means his veins and arteries were switched around from normal. So, the veins were connected to the heart where arteries should have been connected. The arteries connected where veins belonged. That caused problems and he could go into a cardiac arrest at any time without an AAED (automatic external defibrillator). He needed to have one at home and one at his school.

A group of EMTs (emergency medical technicians) heard about Camden's diagnosis and wanted to help. So they started making calls. Within two hours they had an AAED donated and delivered to Camden's home.

The EMTs wanted to do more and thought his family might need training on how to use the device. They volunteered to go to the home and train Camden and his family on their off-duty hours.

The mother, still reeling from the diagnoses and costs involved, cried and expressed her gratitude. The local EMTs have kept up with Camden and his family and visit him. Camden is ten now and doing well. He loves the medics who first took him by ambulance to the hospital.

Bible Story Connection 3–4 minutes

Read Matthew 25:35–40 when Jesus shared about caring for people in need.

Chat Prompts

MORE TIME?

- *Suppose one of you says to them, "Go. I hope everything turns out fine for you. Keep warm. Eat well." And suppose you do nothing about what they really need. Then what good have you done?* James 2:16

   Why is it important to both notice and act on needs? How have members of your family helped people in need?

- *I ask you to receive her as one who belongs to the Lord. Receive her in the way God's people should. Give her any help she may need from you. She has been a great help to many people, including me.* Romans 16:2

   Paul asked friends to help one of his friends. Have you ever asked other people to join in helping someone? Have you taken part in a race or other activity to raise money to help people? What difference does it make when more people help?

- *Suppose someone sees a brother or sister in need and is able to help them. And suppose that person doesn't take pity on these needy people. Then how can the love of God be in that person?* 1 John 3:17

   Discuss compassion and the desire to help someone. When have you felt thankful for someone meeting your needs?

Scrapbook/Prayer Journal Options

Remember how your family serves through adding to your scrapbook or journal.

- Draw eyes and next to them and write what needs you might notice.
- Trace your hand and write how you or your family help(s) others.
- Draw a pot and you making a meal for someone in need.

Frontline Tips

If your family or circle of friends includes any EMTs, ask them to teach you first aid. Ask them to share some stories of people they have helped.

Prayer

Father, help us notice when we can help someone and help us put others first. In Jesus' name, amen.

Wrap-Up

Chat about helping neighbors and friends in need.

Managing Stress

Family Beatitude: Happy is the family who manages stress, for they will function well.

Focus: Identifying and coping with anxiety and worry

Weekly Bible Verse: *Carry one another's heavy loads. If you do, you will fulfill the law of Christ.* Galatians 6:2

Activity Options

- ☐ Make a playlist of songs your family enjoys. Include some praise songs. Chat about how music can lift your spirits.

- ☐ Make a list of what you enjoy doing together that makes everyone smile. Make sure to add one of those activities to stressful days.

- ☐ When everyone feels stressed, call for "silly time." Form a circle and let everyone bend over, drop their arms straight down, and shake their heads. Stand up and see who can make a face that makes everyone laugh.

Frosty Help 2 minutes

Amy Rose walked back into her base office and plopped into her chair. She was exhausted from coping with a string of emergencies. She thought, *It's a tough day. I don't want to be here. I want to be home.*

She heard a beep and looked at her phone. Her daughter, Carolyn, had sent a text, "Heard a lot of sirens today. Are you okay?"

"Tired, but back at the base. It's been rough."

A little while later, Carolyn and her dad, Mike, showed up carrying large, icy soft-serve shakes. They gave one to Amy Rose and one to her partner and each had one of their own. Amy Rose gave her husband and daughter big hugs. Smiling slightly, she said, "I so needed this. I was feeling burned out."

After the last loud slurps, Mike gave her a quick shoulder massage and then prayed for fewer emergencies.

The next day, Amy Rose was off duty, but her firefighter husband was on duty. Amy Rose cooked their family's favorite meal. Amy Rose and Carolyn took food to the fire station and sat to eat with Mike and other firefighters. They shared jokes and stories and laughed.

Later, as they were getting into the car, Carolyn sighed loudly. Amy Rose asked her daughter, "Is something wrong?"

"Well, not really wrong . . . I'm just a little worried. I had a big test today and I'm not sure if I'm going to get a good grade."

Amy Rose put an arm around her daughter. "Look. I know you studied last night for that test. Did you do your best?"

Carolyn nodded. "Then I'm sure everything will be fine. Let's go have some fun and get your mind off that test."

Amy Rose and Carolyn headed to their favorite bookstore to buy some new books and then drove home to play games and read to one another. Before going to bed, they sat and prayed together, thanking God for their family and how they encouraged and supported one another.

Bible Story Connection 3–4 minutes

Read 1 Kings 19:1–8 and discover how
God sent an angel to feed Elijah when he felt stressed. See how much that encouraged and strengthened the prophet.

Chat Prompts

- *If one part suffers, every part suffers with it. If one part is honored, every part shares in its joy.* 1 Corinthians 12:26

    How does your family share their joys and sorrows? How does that help?

- *Give praise to the Lord. Give praise to God our Savior. He carries our heavy loads day after day.* Psalm 68:19

    Discuss giving your worries to God. How can you let go of anxiety?

- *Finally, my brothers and sisters, always think about what is true. Think about what is noble, right and pure. Think about what is lovely and worthy of respect. If anything is excellent or worthy of praise, think about those kinds of things.* Philippians 4:8

    How does thinking about good things and happy memories help you feel less stressed? What are some of your favorite things to think about?

MORE TIME?

147

Scrapbook/Prayer Journal Options

Share how faith helps you feel better and what else helps.

- Draw a circle to represent a stress ball and write about how your family helps one another to de-stress.

- Draw a game piece or toy and write how playing helps you feel happier.

- Write a few favorite jokes to remember that laughter relieves stress.

Frontline Tips

Keep a list of what helps relieve stress for each family member—especially those in a high-stress job. Shower individuals with their stress relievers as needed.

Prayer

Dear Lord, teach our family to support one another and to help relieve stress when we notice a family member has had a difficult day. In Jesus' name, amen.

Wrap-Up

Discuss your best stress relievers.

Communicating through Technology

Family Beatitude: Happy is the family who connects through technology, for they will build bridges of communication.

Focus: Connecting through technology

Weekly Bible Verse: *So let us do all we can to live in peace. And let us work hard to build up one another.* Romans 14:19

Activity Options

☐ Use technology like group texting for those old enough to have phones, and a shared online calendar.

☐ Make use of sticky notes to pass messages to family members, such as when you'll be home or a chore reminder. Place them where they'll be read.

☐ Work on communicating clearly. Play the game of telephone by whispering a message to see how things can get mixed-up. Discuss good communication skills.

Family Group Texting 2 minutes

Lucas's day had been a great big, no-good, terrible mess. He anxiously waited all day to get home and talk to someone in his family. But no one was home!

Lucas decided to set up group texting for his family. He texted a message to each person saying, "We are a family group, so let's use this way to keep up and share our needs."

Everyone responded with emoji smiles or thumbs-up signs. Soon they were using group texting to let everyone in the family know their location and when they planned to arrive home. A simple emoji sad face from one of the children let Mom know to call right away.

Lucas also received texts with his family members, such as when Mom stopped at the store and wanted to know if anyone needed something, or Dad had an unexpected problem that meant his shift as a police officer might go later than planned.

Most of all, the family passed messages to pray, encourage one another, share high-five moments, mention lows, or call a family meeting.

Vicki, Lucas's mom, had modeled the need to communicate well. He'd heard her say "We need to talk" to his dad at times—especially when things seemed tense. They'd set up a time to talk and share their concerns. It eased things at home and laughter filled the house.

Now that Lucas and his siblings were older and all in their teens, it seemed they were always heading out in different directions. He felt better having a way to stay in touch. Fam-texting worked.

Bible Story Connection 3–4 minutes

Read how God connected Peter and Cornelius through visions and messages in Acts 10. Chat about how goodness can communicate faster than technology.

Chat Prompts

- *The hearts of wise people guide their mouths. Their words make people want to learn more.* Proverbs 16:23

  Chat about what your parents taught you in words and actions. How can we wisely communicate?

- *If any of you needs wisdom, you should ask God for it. He will give it to you. God gives freely to everyone and doesn't find fault.* James 1:5

  Chat about ways your family communicates and how well you listen. How does listening matter in learning and communicating?

- *I am about to do something new. It is beginning to happen even now. Don't you see it coming? I am going to make a way for you to go through the desert. I will make streams of water in the dry and empty land.* Isaiah 43:19

  God is the Creator and he plans new things for us. Chat about how God gives us minds to invent or use new technology.

MORE TIME?

Scrapbook/Prayer Journal Options

Create a memory of a time your family communicated well.

- Draw a cell phone and write about how your family communicates.

- Draw the four seasons and how you use calendars to let the family know everyone's plans.

- Draw links and write how communication keeps your family linked.

Frontline Tips

- For separations, use what you can in technology to connect.

- Let the traveler have a duplicate or online copy of a devotional the family will use, so you can communicate on the same topics.

Prayer

Dear Father, help us use new tools and technology for your good and to help our family. In Jesus' name, amen.

Wrap-Up

Name new tools or technology that are helping your family and discuss how they help.

Flexibility

Family Beatitude: Happy is the family who adapts to change, for they will be flexible and not break.

Focus: Encouraging adaptability

Weekly Bible Verse: *We know that in all things God works for the good of those who love him. He appointed them to be saved in keeping with his purpose.* Romans 8:28

Activity Options

☐ Do some bending and stretching exercises to help your body's flexibility.

☐ Put up some obstacles in your home so that people will need to take a different path to the kitchen or other room. Chat about unexpected changes.

☐ Hold up a bendable straw and talk about flexibility and being bendable when something is different. Decorate it to make a flexible straw person.

☐ Try new things to promote flexible thinking and attitudes. Change the daily routine. Even little changes can be fun and encourage flexibility. For example, establish a day when no one can walk or run as normal, but must move differently. Award extra points for creativity!

Broken Routine 2 minutes

Denisa came in the door from work, picked up her two-year-old son and began their bedtime routine. First, they splashed and played with toys in the bathtub. Then D'Vonte grabbed a favorite book. Denisa read that and then a page from his devotional. She tucked him in bed, told him about her day, and said a prayer before kissing him goodnight.

The next morning Denisa said, "Surprise! I'm home all day." D'Vonte whined and wanted his stay-at-home dad, Carl, to do everything. Daddy had to dress him, get his cereal, and play with him.

Carl said, "Let's go to the zoo with mommy. You like the animals." D'Vonte nodded. At the zoo D'Vonte let Mom hold his hand. They laughed at the monkeys and tried to imitate animal sounds.

They went to a restaurant. Carl said prayers and the waiter brought the food. D'Vonte fussed when Mom started to feed him. He wanted Dad. When they returned home, and Mom said it was time for his bath, D'Vonte smiled and went off to his bath.

Denisa sighed and turning to Carl said, "I love serving in the military and enjoy getting days off, but D'Vonte can't get used to a change from his routine."

Carl responded, "Maybe we both need to talk to D'Vonte about the day before you have a day off to try to prepare him." Denisa nodded, smiled, and left to help D'Vonte begin the bedtime routine.

Bible Story Connection 3–4 minutes

Read about Philip in Acts 8:26–40 and learn how following God changed his plans and his attitude.

Chat Prompts

MORE TIME?

- *I know what it's like not to have what I need. I also know what it's like to have more than I need. I have learned the secret of being content no matter what happens. I am content whether I am well fed or hungry. I am content whether I have more than enough or not enough.* Philippians 4:12

    Chat about how being flexible helps you be content and to live with sudden or unpleasant changes.

- *You don't even know what will happen tomorrow. What is your life? It is a mist that appears for a little while. Then it disappears.* James 4:14

    Discuss how our days pass quickly and we should choose to accept change and adapt when things change.

- *The LORD had said to Abram, "Go from your country, your people and your father's family. Go to the land I will show you.* Genesis 12:1

    Talk about big changes like moving, a new grade in school, making new friends, and what's hard, fun, easy, or difficult about changes. Talk about changes that God might ask us to make.

Scrapbook/Prayer Journal Options

Capture memories of keeping faith when changes happen.

- Draw a toothbrush and write about your morning routine.
- Draw a foot or shoe and write about exploring new places.
- Draw a Bible and write about accepting God's plans.

Frontline Tips

- For families with a changing schedule and separations, be willing to choose a new date for celebrating a birthday or holiday.
- For families facing a move, chose a positive attitude and start looking up what the new area is like and what attractions, programs, and parks they have there.

Prayer

Dear Lord, help us be flexible and ready to follow you even if it means accepting change. In Jesus' name, amen.

Wrap-Up

Chat about one change you'd like to make in your home life.

Reunions

Family Beatitude: Happy is the family who reunites with joy for they will be loyal.

Focus: Reunions

Weekly Bible Verse: *The Holy Spirit makes you one in every way. So try your best to remain as one. Let peace keep you together.* Ephesians 4:3

Activity Options

- ☐ Create a special album for each child with photos of them with each family member. If a separation occurs for work, use the album for the child to feel the presence of any absent person.

- ☐ Discuss bedtime routines and what makes your child feel loved. If the usual bedtime caregiver sometimes works late or has odd shifts, consider playing a recorded bedtime message as a voice reunion.

- ☐ Hang up a calendar and help children learn days and weeks. Let them countdown to a special event a few days away or a parent's date with them.

157

Daddy's Home 2 minutes

Every night two-year-old Kaylee and her mom would stand next to her daddy's picture and pray. Mommy would say, "God, be with Daddy while he is away and bring him home safe." Then Kaylee would say, "Goodnight, Daddy," and would kiss his photo.

In the morning, Kaylee would ask, "Daddy home?"

"No, not today. Do you remember watching his ship pull away and float out on the ocean?"

Kaylee nodded.

"Well, we will go back to that place and watch when it is time for Daddy to come back with the ship. He's working and helping to keep people safe."

A few months later, Kaylee and her mom went to the port and watched the ship come in. Kaylee's Dad gave them both a hug and tried to lift Kaylee from her mom's arms. But, Kaylee hid her face and wined a little.

Daddy said, "Kaylee, you forgot me. I'm your daddy. I have a present for you." He held out a stuffed fish. Kaylee grabbed the fish and clutched it tight.

At home, she kept her distance from her dad. That evening, Daddy laid on the bed while Kaylee and her mom got her ready for bed by saying prayers. After praying, Kaylee ran to the photo of her dad, said, "Goodnight, Daddy," and kissed the photo.

Daddy said, "Goodnight, Kaylee."

Kaylee looked at him. Then she looked back at the photo and then at her daddy. She looked at the photo again and then turned to her daddy. Suddenly, she yelled, "Daddy's home!" and jumped on the bed to give her daddy a big hug.

Bible Story Connection 3–4 minutes

Read John 20:11–18 about how Mary did not recognize Jesus after the resurrection until he spoke to her. How has someone seemed different after you've been apart for a while?

Chat Prompts

MORE TIME?

- *That's the way it is with you. Now it's your time to be sad. But I will see you again. Then you will be full of joy. And no one will take away your joy.* John 16:22

  Discuss how it's good to see someone again when you've been apart.

- *Do your best to come to me quickly.* 2 Timothy 4:9

  Discuss how people who travel for work really want to return home as soon as possible. List reasons why they need to be away.

- *Look up. Look all around you. All your people are getting together to come back to you. Your sons will come from far away. Your daughters will be carried on the hip like little children.* Isaiah 60:4

  This scripture is part of a Psalm about a reunion with God. Chat about how God wants all people to come to him.

Scrapbook/Prayer Journal Options

Add art and words to remember how God keeps a family united.

- Draw wheels or propellers and write about trips a family member might take for work.

- Draw arms and write about welcome-home hugs.

- Draw a Bible and write how prayer and scriptures keep people united in their hearts and minds.

Frontline Tips

- Encourage children to write a short list of what they want the absent family member to do when they return (hugs, favorite game, special outing). Mail it to the person far away.

- When a family member is away, talk about what will happen when they return. Talk about when you expect the return.

Prayer

Dear Lord, we pray for families who must be apart because of military deployments and other work commitments. We ask that you keep them united in their love. In Jesus' name, amen.

Wrap-Up

Chat about reunions and what makes them special.

Praying Together

Family Beatitude: Happy is the family who prays together, for they will be close.

Focus: Practicing family prayer

Weekly Bible Verse: *Where two or three people gather in my name, I am there with them.* Matthew 18:20

Activity Options

☐ Find a place in your home where it's easy to gather to pray (table, couches, floor, etc.) and make that your prayer war room.

☐ Hang a white board in your prayer war room for people to write their prayer needs.

☐ For young ones, you can have a prayer lamb or other stuffed animal to pass to the next person to pray. Encourage your little ones to keep the prayer lamb in the prayer war room and go there at times to pray quietly.

The War Room 2 minutes

Lex entered the house and yelled, "I need everyone in the war room." Everyone stopped what they were doing and filed into the family room. They gathered in a circle, plopping down on pillows. Lex explained that there was an accident during baseball practice and his best friend had a concussion and possibly a broken arm.

His mom asked a few questions to find out more about what happened. Lex's friend had slipped on home plate and fell backward. He hit his head so hard that he passed out. Once everyone knew the situation, their mom started the prayer. When she was done praying, she squeezed the hand of her daughter, who was seated to her right. Prayers continued around the circle, with each person either praying out loud or silently, and then squeezing the hand of the next person. Lex's dad, the last person in the circle, closed the prayer.

After the prayer time the family gave Lex a group hug.

Sloan said, "I'm glad we saw the movie that gave us the idea of a war room." The family had moved furniture around to clear an area and bought several large pillows, so they could kneel or sit and feel comfy. "I like praying together whenever we need it."

Mom said, "We always asked each other at meals to pray, but this is much better."

Lex's dad said, "I'm thankful I was home this time, and not off on call. Let's add a white board on the wall to write prayer needs. Anyone missing can catch up later and pray."

Bible Story Connection 3–4 minutes

Read about friends of Jesus gathering in a house to pray together in Acts 1:13–14, 2:1–4 and discover how God filled them with the Holy Spirit as they prayed.

Chat Prompts

MORE TIME?

- *So confess your sins to one another. Pray for one another so that you might be healed. The prayer of a godly person is powerful. Things happen because of it.* James 5:16

   Discuss what has happened when you have prayed.

- *The believers studied what the apostles taught. They shared their lives together. They ate and prayed together.* Acts 2:42

   Chat about how praying together can be as easy as sharing meals or doing other things together.

- *Cornelius and all his family were faithful and worshiped God. He gave freely to people who were in need. He prayed to God regularly.* Acts 10:2

   Chat about how your family prays and how prayer helps us be more kind and more generous. What does faithful mean?

Scrapbook/Prayer Journal Options

Describe prayer memories in words and/or art.

- Draw a circle and write about praying together.

- Draw an ear and write about listening to prayer needs.

- Draw a cross and write about how Jesus is with your family as you pray together.

Frontline Tips

- When a family member deploys make a list of ways to pray for that person. Also list other prayers that God answered while the family member was away.

- Send a prayer card each week summing up the family prayers to the absent family member.

Prayer

Dear Lord Jesus, we are grateful that you are with us when we pray. Bless us with answers. In your name, amen.

Wrap-Up

Discuss the best things about praying as a family.

Grace in a Fishbowl

Family Beatitude: Happy is the family who lives authentically for they see God's grace at work.

Focus: Sharing God's grace in daily life

Weekly Bible Verse: *All this is for your benefit. God's grace is reaching more and more people. So they will become more and more thankful. They will give glory to God.* 2 Corinthians 4:15

Activity Options

☐ When someone hurts you, forgive and do something kind like give a compliment to the person.

☐ Have some popcorn with no salt or other seasoning. Then try some that is seasoned. What's the difference? Compare plain, dry toast and cinnamon toast. Chat about how words are better when seasoned with grace.

☐ Post notes of how people have shown grace to members of your family.

You're So Real 2 minutes

Sheri looked around at the mess when the doorbell rang. She called to her children to stop fighting as she answered the door.

Jada and Betty were at the door. Both were new to the ministry of Officer's Christian Fellowship. They had time off from their college studies to come visit. Sheri apologized for the children's books and items that composed the mess and for the shouting from their rooms.

Betty laughed and said, "It makes me feel at home. You have an interesting house with so many windows."

Sheri laughed, "Anyone walking by can see inside. It's a fishbowl!"

Jada looked out toward the front yard. "Is that someone you know? Or is a stranger out front picking your flowers?"

Sherri dashed outside and asked the stranger, "Excuse me, what are you doing with my flowers?"

"I saw the ministry sign and figured that you wouldn't mind if I helped myself to some of your pretty flowers."

Sherri took a deep breath and said, "Those are for the use of the ministry. I'd love to share a little about what we do to help students and military families."

The woman turned without a word, and left, clutching the flowers she had picked.

Betty stood at the doorway and said, "It must be hard to live like this."

Sheri's youngest daughter grinned and said, "Mommy meets lots of people this way and tells them about Jesus. She says that's passing on God's grace. One woman came back last week and thanked mommy because now she loves Jesus."

Bible Story Connection 3–4 minutes

Read Romans 5:1–2, 15–17 and discuss how Christ's gift of grace means we will be in heaven one day and his grace makes us right with God.

Chat Prompts

- *God's grace has saved you because of your faith in Christ. Your salvation doesn't come from anything you do. It is God's gift.* Ephesians 2:8

  Discuss how we don't deserve heaven, but God extends grace and saves us. What did he do? *Charis* is the Greek word in the New Testament for grace. It means favor, blessing, or kindness. It's making a choice to bless someone who does not deserve it. How have you done that?

- *May God our Father and the Lord Jesus Christ give you grace and peace.* 1 Corinthians 1:3

  Why do we want grace and peace and why should we want others to have them, too?

- *You do well in everything else. You do well in faith and in speaking. You do well in knowledge and in complete commitment. And you do well in the love we have helped to start in you. So make sure that you also do well in the grace of giving to others.* 2 Corinthians 8:7

  Grace is talked about with love, faith, and even speech. How can our speech, the words we say, give grace to others?

Scrapbook/Prayer Journal Options

Remember your family's chats about grace with art and/or words.

- ☐ Draw a cross and write about God's grace.
- ☐ Draw a face and write words of kindness that you can use to show grace.
- ☐ Draw a salt shaker and write about how grace makes life better.

Frontline Tips

- ☐ Sometimes people can say hurtful things to police or other people who serve. Be extra kind with words to your family members who serve others.
- ☐ Make a praise poster about the ways the members of your family serve others and hang it up where everyone can see it.

Prayer

Dear Lord, thanks for your grace that saved us. Help us extend grace to others. In Jesus' name, amen.

Wrap-Up

Chat about how Christ's gift of grace saves us.

Healing Actions and Words

Family Beatitude: Happy is the family who experiences healing, for they will believe in miracles.

Focus: Healing actions and words

Weekly Bible Verse: *He heals those who have broken hearts. He takes care of their wounds.* Psalm 147:3

Activity Options

☐ Rub some aloe vera or other soothing cream on your skin and chat about how it's a medicinal balm that helps heal and takes the sting away from insect and other bites. Mix body glitter with aloe vera gel for a sparkling, soothing gel.

☐ Look up pictures of jellyfish. The long tentacles are invisible in the water and can cause a lot of pain. Find out when it is jellyfish season in your area and avoid swimming during those times.

☐ Practice staying calm even when in pain. Take slow, deep breathes, and listen as a care-giver explains what is happening and the steps they will take to help you feel better.

Man-of-War Sting 2 minutes

A mother rushed into the fire station carrying her screaming son Joey. He had been enjoying the waves and swimming in the ocean when suddenly he began howling in pain.

Lieutenant Tommy Neimann, a firefighter and EMT, noticed the red marks Joey's leg indicated that a man-of-war, a jelly-fish like creature must have stung him. Tommy told Joey's mother, "He'll be OK."

Joey continued screaming at full volume until another firefighter said, "Here's a cookie if you can stop crying."

Joey reached for the cookie and calmed down as he chewed.

Tommy gently swabbed a solution of warm water and ammonia on the sting marks to sooth the pain.

Joey noticed the men cooking lunch and said, "I like hot dogs, too."

Soon Joey started chomping on a hot dog in a bun. He nodded when Tommy said, "I bet you were having all kinds of fun until that mean jellyfish stung you."

Joey's mom said to her son, "Since your booboo is all better, it's time to go. Say thank you and tell the nice firemen goodbye."

Joey started feeling pain again and asked Tommy to rub the cloth on his leg some more. He settled down again. Joey's mom smiled, thanked the men for their help, lifted her son, and left.

Bible Story Connection 3–4 minutes

Read Luke 10:25-31 which tells the story of a good person who helped an injured man. He's called a Good Samaritan. EMTS, doctors, and nurses help injured people, too.

Chat Prompts

MORE TIME?

- *A cheerful heart makes you healthy. But a broken spirit dries you up.* Proverbs 17:22

  How does being cheerful make you feel better?

- *News about [Jesus] spread all over Syria. People brought to him all who were ill with different kinds of sicknesses. Some were suffering great pain. Others were controlled by demons. Some were shaking wildly. Others couldn't move at all. And Jesus healed all of them.* Matthew 4:24

  Chat about the Jesus' ability to heal people.

- *The words of thoughtless people cut like swords. But the tongue of wise people brings healing.* Proverbs 12:18

  How do kind words help you feel better?
  Chat about sympathy and compassion.

Scrapbook/Prayer Journal Options

Journal about how God has blessed your family with healing and health.

- Draw a jellyfish and write about times you have been hurt.

- Draw a smiley face and talk about how kind words help you feel better.

- Draw a hand and write about how EMTs, nurses, and doctors use their hands to help heal others.

Frontline Tips

- Listen when medical workers share their good feelings of helping to heal someone or their bad feelings of being unable to help. Pray with them and remember that God is the true healer so it's OK when they can't heal everyone.

- Wear a bandage as a reminder to pray for those who help with medical injuries.

Prayer

Thank you, Father, for men and women who work hard to heal people and rescue those who are injured. In Jesus' name, amen.

Wrap-Up

Chat about the job of emergency workers and how God is the great healer.

172

Faith First

Family Beatitude: Happy is the family that makes faith a priority for they will believe in the Lord.

Focus: Putting faith first

Weekly Bible Verse: *Make sure your children learn [God's commands]. Talk about them when you are at home. Talk about them when you walk along the road. Speak about them when you go to bed. And speak about them when you get up.* Deuteronomy 6:7

Activity Options

☐ Have a Bible beside the dinner table so that it's easy to link meal-time topics to Scripture.

☐ Each week, post a Scripture from a sermon and be sure to discuss it. Ask family members to share how they apply that Scripture to situations that they face.

☐ Post a picture of a flourishing tree. Add notes on it of how each family member has grown in their faith.

Anytime Faith 2 minutes

Vicki and Doug pulled into their favorite restaurant for their weekly outing after church. The children climbed out of the van and chatted about what they planned to order. Once they had their food, Doug asked them to share what they learned at church that morning.

Susie said, "We learned about a mustard seed and how it grows to be a big tree. Our faith can grow, too."

They launched in a discussion about how faith had grown in each family member. Susie said, "One of my friends does family devotions every day, but we don't."

Vicki smiled and explained, "Since Dad's police duty changes all the time, our schedule has made daily devotions difficult. So we chose to weave faith into our lives. You see us open the Bible during lots of discussions. We even share Scriptures when doing homework on topics like science. We make sure we take time to read and talk about a Bible passage every few days. It's just not very planned scheduled."

Susie's older brother said, "I like it that way. I know I can ask about God and faith any old time. It seems like a natural part of my daily life."

Bible Story Connection 3–4 minutes

Read Hebrews 11:1–12 about what faith means and how Bible people showed their faith. Why do you think this chapter is called the hall of faith?

Chat Prompts

- *The Berean Jews were very glad to receive Paul's message. They studied the Scriptures carefully every day. They wanted to see if what Paul said was true. So they were more noble than the Thessalonians Jews.* Acts 17:11

  Talk about ways to study the Bible and what helps you understand the words.

- *I remember your honest and true faith. It was alive first in your grandmother Lois and in your mother Eunice. And I am certain that it is now alive in you also.* 2 Timothy 1:5

  Discuss how your parents learned about God and the importance of sharing faith as a family.

- *[Jesus] replied, "Suppose you have faith as small as a mustard seed. Then you can say to this mulberry tree, 'Be pulled up. Be planted in the sea.' And it will obey you."* Luke 17:6

  Look at a mustard seed, if possible. It's very tiny. Chat about why faith matters and how you have grown in faith.

Scrapbook/Prayer Journal Options

Create memory pages about your family's faith.

- Draw seeds and a tree. Write about growing your faith.

- Draw a Bible and write favorite verses or lessons learned.

- Draw a magnifying glass and write ways to study God's Word.

Frontline Tips

- Be flexible if a family member has a rotating or changing schedule. Find ways to connect with faith and converse about God and Scriptures.

- Share Scriptures by text.

Prayer

Dear Lord, thanks for the gift of the Bible. Help us understand what we read and study and help us grow in our faith. In Jesus' name, amen.

Wrap-Up

Share one way you grew in faith recently.

Beloved Messages

Family Beatitude: Happy is the family who shares words of love, for they will feel treasured.

Focus: Recording words of love and comfort

Weekly Bible Verse: *I was very worried. But your comfort brought me joy.* Psalm 94:19

Activity Options

☐ If you know someone who has a family member gone for long periods of time, make them some cards with funny jokes and a nice note to comfort them.

☐ If a close family member travels or works nights and is away when a child wakes up, keep the person's photo next to the child's bed in a frame that includes a voice message.

☐ Make a list of anxiety busters to use as needed: exercise, extra hugs, coloring, puzzles, singing, visualizing a calm place, remembering a happy time, self-pep phrases like *It will be okay* or *I can do this.*

My Daddy Doll 2 minutes

Ethan clutched a stuffed pillow as he entered his classroom dressed in pajamas. Today the students all came in pajamas for a dress-up day. The teacher asked Ethan to show his pillow and talk about it.

He held it up and everyone saw the pillow had a picture of a man in an Air Force uniform. He said, "This is my daddy pillow and it's my dad in his uniform. When I press here he speaks to me." Ethan pressed the pillow and the class listened to Ethan's dad say how much he loved Ethan and that he'd come home as soon as he could.

The teacher asked about his dad and Ethan said he had to go away for his job for many weeks, but he'd be back soon. His teacher talked about family members who travel for work and how some had to be away a long time.

Ethan added, "I miss him and feel sad at bedtime, because when he's home, he always reads me a story. But hearing his voice makes me feel better. Mom, my sister, and I are staying with my grandpa and grandma while Daddy is away."

When Ethan's dad returned, Ethan was so happy to have his dad pick him up from school and meet his teacher.

Bible Story Connection 3–4 minutes

Read Matthew 6:26–34 and chat about letting go of worries.

Chat Prompts

MORE TIME?

- *I have a lot to write to you. But I don't want to use paper and ink. I hope I can visit you instead. Then I can talk with you face to face. That will make our joy complete.* 2 John 12

  Discuss how family members miss one another and long to have time together. Chat about what activities you enjoy as a family.

- *Love is patient. Love is kind. It does not want what belongs to others. It does not brag. It is not proud.* 1 Corinthians 13:4

  Discuss what helps you wait for a family member to return. How can you be patient? How does your family's love help you be happy with what you have?

- *Turn all your worries over to him. He cares about you.* 1 Peter 5:7

  Chat about giving worries to God and being less anxious. What can you do when you feel worried?

Scrapbook/Prayer Journal Options

Add memories about comfort.

- Draw a favorite stuffed animal and write about comfort.

- Draw some tears and write about what cheers up different family members.

- Write notes of love to one another, so that your scrapbook will also be a reminder of how your family members love one another.

Frontline Tips

- Before a parent deploys, buy a special stuffed animal to comfort each child.

- Write some notes and buy little surprises that can be placed in the paws of the stuffed animals weekly.

Prayer

Lord, comfort children as they miss an absent family member and help them be patient in waiting for their return. In Jesus' name, amen.

Wrap-Up

Chat about what brings comfort to you and how you give comfort to others.

Respect and Honor

Family Beatitude: Happy is the family that always shows respect, for they will develop a good reputation.

Focus: Showing respectfulness and valuing people

Weekly Bible Verse: *Do not make something wrong appear to be right. Treat poor people and rich people in the same way. Do not favor one person over another. Instead, judge everyone fairly.* Leviticus 19:15

Activity Options

- [ ] Hold up a deflated balloon. Talk about respect and how it helps. Ask for examples, such as, someone asked for your help, thanked you, or complimented you. For each example, blow air into the balloon. Then talk about how disrespect hurts. Ask for examples again, such as someone shoved you and snickered, no one seems to care about your feelings, someone spread a rumor about you, someone grabbed something from you without asking. For each example of disrespect, let a little air out of the balloon. Explain that respect can build up a person like blowing up a balloon. But disrespect can deflate someone like letting the air out of the balloon. Give everyone a balloon and take turns acting out ways to be respectful. The person shown respect blows air in their balloon. Continue until everyone's balloon is filled.

- [ ] Keep a dish of mints out as representative that good and respectful words are as nice as minty breath. If someone is respectful, offer them a mint as reinforcement of their sweet words.

- [ ] Adults, model respect. Let children catch the men in their family opening doors for the women, the women serving a snack to someone who just came home from work or school, or other respectful actions.

- [ ] Stop a child who complains about an adult in the family and say, "Hold on. You're talking about someone I love. He (She)'s wonderful and (list one praiseworthy action or ability)."

Don't Ticket My Friend's Parents! 2 minutes

The call rang out. "Dad's home!"

The kids ran to the front door. They waited for their dad to remove his holster, lock it up, and then wrapped him in hugs.

"Dad, did you capture bad guys?"

"No. I had traffic duty today. Just a few tickets and broken headlights."

Bret said, "I hope you didn't stop any of my friends' parents. They'd get mad at me if one of their parents gets a ticket. They think giving people tickets is mean."

"Well, I don't go to work to be mean. I want to keep roads safe so people avoid accidents and getting hurt. Everyone I stopped remained calm. I spoke gently and showed them respect. The people I ticketed took it like medicine."

"Ugh. I don't like medicine."

"But medicine is needed, and sometimes so is a ticket or warning."

Mom called, "Hey, everyone, look at the news."

They strolled into the family room and listened as a reporter interviewed a man in Arizona who praised police officers. The officers had stopped him for a broken headlight. It made the news because the police officer was white, and the man was

182

African American and carried a gun. The man posted online about the courtesy of the police and his own choice to be respectful. The officers gave him a warning.

"Cool," said Bret. "Maybe kids at school will see this and be nice."

Dad said, "That would be good. I still have a job to do. I want to keep people safe, and that means everyone."

Bret gave his dad a bear hug.

Bible Story Connection 3–4 minutes

Read Ephesians 6:5–9 and Romans 13:1.
Chat about respect.

Chat Prompts

- *You should want a good name more than you want great riches. To be highly respected is better than having silver or gold.* Proverbs 22:1

    Chat about becoming a person who is worthy of respect. Why does it matter?

MORE TIME?

- *Give to everyone what you owe them. Do you owe taxes? Then pay them. Do you owe anything else to the government? Then pay it. Do you owe respect? Then give it. Do you owe honor? Then show it.* Romans 13:7

    Chat about why every person God created should be given respect. How does showing respect to God's people also show respect for God?

- *Praise the LORD. Blessed are those who have respect for the LORD. They find great delight when they obey God's commands.* Psalm 112:1

    Why is it important to respect rules? What rules help us respect people's property? What rules do police enforce? Why are they important?

Scrapbook/Prayer Journal Options

Bring art to the pages to depict respect.

- Draw inflated balloons and words of respect.

- Draw deflated balloons and reasons people feel disrespected.

- Draw a Bible on a shelf or place of honor.

Frontline Tips

- Talk about being like Jesus when people are hurtful or disrespectful because of your work. On a paper cross, write a prayer asking God to forgive the ones who caused the hurt and to heal the hurt family member.

- If you are in a service position that is sometimes ridiculed, remind your family of the mission behind your service. Explain why your mission is important and why some people get angry.

Prayer

Father, you are worthy of my respect. Help me respect the people you created and help me be worthy of respect.

Wrap-Up

Discuss what you learned about respect this week and why it's important to respect people.

Art Therapy

Family Beatitude: Happy is the family that encourages children to express their feelings in art for they will learn to release fears and worries.

Focus: Art therapy

Weekly Bible Verse: *Lord, you have made so many things! How wise you were when you made all of them! The earth is full of your creatures.* Psalm 104:24

Activity Options

- ☐ Keep art supplies on hand so children can use art therapy to release emotions. Ask them to describe the drawings so you'll understand what they are thinking and feeling.

- ☐ For busy artists who draw a lot, make some of their collections into books. Staple or bind them.

- ☐ Look at illustrations in books and talk about how the art helps us understand and remember the story.

FAMILY DEVOTION · READ ALOUD ·

Red Grass 2 minutes

Lynn answered the phone when she saw the number of her daughter's school.

Becky's teacher said, "I wanted to speak to you while I know Becky is in school. I'm concerned about her because of a drawing. Many times, children express fear and things when they color. She drew a picture of grass with red all over the grass. I wonder if it represents blood. I know her dad's a firefighter and sees some tough things."

Lynn suppressed a laugh. She explained that just before her husband left to fight wildfires in another state, he made a special rocker for Becky, which they spray painted red. "The grass is still red, and Becky loves to talk about what they might make and paint when he returns. It's her way of dealing with Daddy leaving."

The teacher laughed and said, "That's a relief. I imagine the lawn looks quite special to her and gives her a happy memory."

Later, Lynn picked up Becky from school. Her daughter showed her the picture and chatted happily about painting the grass and rocker with Daddy.

Becky said, "I love my daddy. He likes to make things with me. When I get home, I'll sit in my rocker and read. I might go out and roll in the red grass. That will feel like Daddy is hugging me. I know it will grow and be mowed away soon, but I also know Daddy will put out the fires and come home again."

Bible Story Connection 3–4 minutes

Read John 8:1–11 and chat about Jesus writing in the dirt
when others wanted to stone a woman and trip him up. Talk
about how you have played, built, or drawn in sand.

Chat Prompts

- *She chooses wool and flax. She loves to work
  with her hands.* Proverbs 31:13

    Chat about how God gave us talents and work
    we can do with our hands. Why does doing
    work or making art help us feel better?

- *So Jacob set up a stone as a way to remember.* Genesis 31:45

    Discuss how even a rock can be a reminder to think of God.

- *The LORD has filled Bezalel and Oholiab with skill to do all
  kinds of work. They can carve things and make patterns. They
  can sew skillfully with blue, purple and bright red yarn and on
  fine linen. They use thread to make beautiful cloth. Both of them
  have the skill to work in all kinds of crafts.* Exodus 35:35

    Discuss how our creativity and talent
    for art also comes from God.

Scrapbook/Prayer Journal Options

Add memories of family fun or art activities.

- Draw a paintbrush and write about using art to express feelings.

- Add a rainbow and write about God's art.

- Draw a favorite activity that children like doing with the family member who may be away.

Frontline Tips

- Send a note to teachers if a family member is being deployed or something else is happening at home (new baby, family member death, etc.) so they will understand a child might behave differently.

- When a family member is deployed, consider enrolling children in an art class. They might discover a new outlet for their feelings.

Prayer

Thank you, Lord, for art and the ability to draw and write about our feelings. In Jesus' name, amen.

Wrap-Up

Discuss favorite art and how you feel when you see something beautiful.

Hope of Understanding

Family Beatitude: Happy is the family with children who show understanding, for they will share hope.

Focus: Elevating understanding

Weekly Bible Verse: *A crowd came together when they heard the sound. They were bewildered because each of them heard their own language being spoken.* Acts 2:6

Activity Options

- [ ] Make a chart listing the talents of family members that can be used to bring hope to others. It might include laughter, listening well, cheering people up, or skills like home repairs, sewing, medical aid, etc.

- [ ] Play charades and discuss how hard it can be to communicate when you don't know the other person's language.

- [ ] If a nursing home allows it, make tray favors for the people there to bring them hope and encourage them to smile.

Out of the Shadows 2 minutes

Peggy Sue encouraged her daughter's dream of working in the medical field. Amy Rose wanted to help people and they had found an opportunity for her to shadow an orthopedic doctor in an emergency room. She watched as an ambulance brought in a grandfather who needed immediate surgery.

The man's young grandson was with him when the accident happened. As the EMTs rushed the grandfather to the emergency room, the boy's mother arrived. Both the mother and the boy were deaf and struggled to understand the doctor's explanation.

The doctor mumbled, "Doesn't anyone know sign language?"

Amy Rose stepped forward. "I can interpret." She felt so nervous that her hands shook, but the mother held her wrists, so she could sign. The doctor and mother understood one another through Amy Rose.

That evening Amy Rose rushed into her home and yelled, "I really helped today." She shared her experience and added, "The hospital put me on a call list to interpret when needed." She also admitted how seeing people hurt made her feel scared, but she still wanted to help with emergencies. Her mother prayed with her and thanked God for using her.

As Amy Rose grew up and studied to be an EMT (Emergency Medical Technician), she'd call her mother to talk when she had a tough case or to cry with her about trauma she witnessed. Peggy Sue would pray with her or read a Scripture and remind her that Amy Rose's help gave people hope.

190

Bible Story Connection 3–4 minutes

Read Luke 22:47–51 when Peter cut off a man's ear and Jesus immediately healed the man.

Chat Prompts

- *Lord, you hear the desires of those who are hurting. You cheer them up and give them hope. You listen to their cries.* Psalm 10:17

  Chat about how God listens and understands our fears and gives us hope. How is this important to people who work in hospitals and help with emergencies?

- *Our hope is certain. It is something for the soul to hold on to. It is strong and secure. It goes all the way into the Most Holy Room behind the curtain.* Hebrews 6:19

  Discuss hope and how we need hope. How can we help other people have hope?

- *That belief and understanding lead to the hope of eternal life. Before time began, God promised to give that life. And he does not lie.* Titus 1:2

  Talk about how understanding the needs of others can give them hope. How does our faith give us hope?

Scrapbook/Prayer Journal Options

Create memory pages about your family's hope in God.

- Draw an ear and a mouth and write about understanding.
- Draw an anchor and write about hope.
- Draw a stethoscope and write about healing.

Frontline Tips

- People who work in emergencies see lots of suffering. Pray for them and share Scriptures to remind them of hope.
- Blow bubbles with them as a reminder that God will lift up our worries and lighten our load.

Prayer

Dear Lord, thank you for people who work in the medical field. Help them remain calm as they face traumas. In Jesus' name, amen.

Wrap-Up

Chat about one way to understand another person.

192

Disaster Relief

Family Beatitude: Happy is the family that leans on outside help, for God will bring people to meet their needs.

Focus: Supporting disaster relief

Weekly Bible Verse: *My God will meet all your needs. He will meet them in keeping with his wonderful riches. These riches come to you because you belong to Christ Jesus.* Philippians 4:19

Activity Options

☐ Disaster case managers in many organizations help with recovery and that includes repairing damaged homes. You can help by sending needed items. You can even send gift cards for hardware and appliance stores.

☐ Find out about disaster and flood buckets that churches and organizations collect to send to disaster areas. Make one as a family and donate it. Add in a note of encouragement and a prayer for the family who will receive it.

☐ Disasters can be terrible and it can take a long time for people to recover from them. Write to a church in a disaster area and ask if you can bake and send cookies for a Sunday service. Showing that others care will relieve stress.

Baby's New Room 2 minutes

Vernon showed up at a Federal Emergency Management Agency (FEMA) transition meeting. No options remained. His family needed help. They were expecting a new baby, and everything they own had been damaged, destroyed, or demolished by Hurricane Irma.

At the meeting, Vernon listened to Carrie speak about support from United Methodist Committee on Relief (UMCOR) and felt he could approach her. Carrie listened and said, "We can open a case for you and I'm sure we'll find help."

The next day Carrie's coworker opened a case for Vernon and sent Jim, the contract manager, to meet with him. Meanwhile, Carrie received a call from a church that had raised money they wanted to divide between three national disasters, including Hurricane Irma. They wanted to be involved in choosing the recipient.

Jim realized that the money from Vernon's various sources of relief and insurance fell short of what the family needed. When Jim discussed the situation with Carrie, she decided to share the need with the church she'd heard from. The church approved donating $20,000 to help with Vernon's home—especially because of the needs of the new baby.

The disaster inside the house meant they would have to rebuild every room. Jim and Vernon agreed: a clean room for the baby remained the most pressing need. If they could not provide an approved room for the baby, social services might take the child away.

Jim didn't have a volunteer group coming in from churches that week, so he gathered the UMCOR team while Vernon asked his neighbors and church members to donate some hours. That week, the volunteers laid a new floor, drywall, painted, and decorated the baby's room. Mom and new baby boy arrived home from the hospital to a beautiful, new and safe room.

Bible Story Connection 3–4 minutes

Read Acts 27:37–28:2 and Acts 28:10–11 about a disastrous shipwreck and relief help from the people in the area. The storm broke the boat, but the natives later supplied the survivors with all they needed and three months later they sailed away.

Chat Prompts

- *When you hope, be joyful. When you suffer, be patient. When you pray, be faithful.* Romans 12:12

  Discuss being patient when you have problems or big struggles and what it means to be joyful.

- *To many people I am an example of how much you care. You are my strong place of safety.* Psalm 71:7

  How does accepting help let others see people care about you?

- *God is fair. He will not forget what you have done. He will remember the love you have shown him. You showed it when you helped his people. And you show it when you keep on helping them.* Hebrews 6:10

  Chat about how you have been helped by other people. How is helping one another part of being in God's family?

MORE TIME?

Scrapbook/Prayer Journal Options

Add memory pages about having faith even in hard times.

- Draw a bucket and items that you can put in one to help people in disaster areas.

- Draw some pennies and write about how God's family can give money that adds up to a lot.

- Draw storm clouds and write a Scripture on trusting God in hard times.

Frontline Tips

- For families who have members working in disaster relief, pray that God will supply volunteers, funds, and the supplies needed.

- Make your family member a stress ball. Cut the top off one small balloon and squeeze in a long thin piece of play dough. Alternatively, you could use a funnel and fill a balloon with flour. Knot the balloon's neck, place the filled balloon inside another balloon, and knot it closed. You can decorate the outer balloon with marker drawings before filling it.

Prayer

Lord, help us reach out to give aid to people in disaster areas and for people in our community who have suffered from a catastrophe. In Jesus' name, amen.

Wrap-Up

Chat about a disaster and what's happening to help people there.

God's Guidance

Family Beatitude: Happy is the family who prays for guidance, for they will find direction.

Focus: Seeking God's guidance and outdoor safety

Weekly Bible Verse: *When [Jesus'] parents saw him, they were amazed. His mother said to him, "Son, why have you treated us like this? Your father and I have been worried about you. We have been looking for you everywhere."* Luke 2:48

Activity Options

☐ Discuss and write out safety rules for different activities. For example, when going to an amusement park, determine what to do if someone gets lost, and where to meet at the end of a ride.

☐ Help children write a prayer list or draw pictures for a prayer list.

☐ Help children learn to pay attention to their surroundings and where their parents are.

☐ Look at the sky together and talk about where the sun is during the day and what clouds tell us about the weather.

☐ Try the following:

　○ When giving a child safety directions, have the child repeat them.

　○ As you go to new places, stop and have each person describe things they see.

197

○ When driving a car, ask children to look for landmarks or tell you sounds they hear.

FAMILY DEVOTION · READ ALOUD ·

Lost at the Fair 2 minutes

"Julia! Julia! Julia!" Jennifer yelled frantically.

While her daughter was playing in the bounce house, Jennifer helped a boy who was hurt. When she turned back and looked inside for her daughter, the bounce house was empty.

Jennifer felt the panic begin to rise and yelled louder. Jennifer's husband, David, heard the yelling and started to pray. He felt God whisper to go to the parking lot. David raced to the lot and found his little girl wandering around.

Julia ran to her father and said, "I was trying to find you, Daddy." He lifted her high and hugged her tight.

He reminded her, "You were supposed to stay with Mommy and not follow other children out a different way. Let's go find Mommy. She's worried and looking for you."

David, a policeman patrol officer in New York, trusted God to lead him to missing and lost people. God guides him to find criminals and missing persons.

Every day, Julia prays, "Please, God, keep my daddy safe." She's happy to know he can find the bad people and also find lost children. She knows that since God let him find her, then he can find other children.

Bible Story Connection 3–4 minutes

Read Luke 15:3–7 and talk about how Jesus is like a shepherd who cares for us when we wander off.

Chat Prompts

MORE TIME?

- *The Son of Man came to look for the lost and save them.* Luke 19:10

   Chat about how Jesus looks for people who are lost, people who don't know him. How does Jesus save them?

- *I will search for the lost. I will bring back those who have wandered away. I will bandage the ones who are hurt. I will make the weak ones stronger. But I will destroy those who are fat and strong. I will take good care of my sheep. I will treat them fairly.* Ezekiel 34:16

   Discuss how Jesus cares about every person. How does he make you stronger?

- *"This son of mine was dead. And now he is alive again. He was lost. And now he is found." So they began to celebrate.* Luke 15:24

   Discuss celebrating that you believe in Jesus. Talk about how God celebrates when we believe in him.

Scrapbook/Prayer Journal Options

Add art and words about God's love and care.

- Draw a lamb and write about how Jesus loves you.

- Draw a police badge or hat and write about finding someone who is lost.

- Draw a cross and write about trusting God.

Frontline Tips

- Use encouraging words to honor the law enforcement workers in your family and other families.

- If you have a family member in law enforcement, join a peace officer Christian fellowship organization. You can learn about these organizations by searching online for "Christian law enforcement fellowship."

- If you don't have a law enforcement member in your family, adopt one at Adopt-A-Cop. You can send kind notes and pray for that person. You might also join Badge of Hope Ministries. You can find both organizations online.

Prayer

Lord, protect the people who serve to keep peace in our country. Please bless their families, too. In Jesus' name, amen.

Wrap-Up

Chat about good things police officers do to keep us safe.

Memorials

Family Beatitude: Happy is the family who creates good memories for they will be grateful.

Focus: Remembering and honoring people who served

Weekly Bible Verse: *Those who do what is right will always be secure. They will be remembered forever.* Psalm 112:6

Activity Options

☐ Do some gravestone or other rubbings and discuss people who have gone to heaven. Look at how the rubbings pick up the impression from the engraving. Discuss good impressions people make in life.

☐ Check out Adopt-A-Cop online. Decide if your family will commit to pray every day for a law enforcement officer. You can even send cards that will be delivered to your cop.

☐ Use black paper and red, white, and yellow colored circles to make traffic lights. Punch a hole in the top and string yarn to wear it. Chat about obeying laws.

At the Wall 2 minutes

Nina stood at the Police Memorial Wall with her daughters, touching her late husband's name. They took paper and did a rubbing over the name. They hugged and cried and then went to a grassy area to sit. They talked about the good times with their dad.

A woman walked up and said, "Hello. I'm Kristi and this is my husband Rick. We're with Badge of Hope and we're so sorry for your loss." They joined the family and the little girls climbed on Rick's lap. They started to put leaves and grass in his hair and he laughed with them. They shared good memories about their dad. Kristi listened to Nina share her story.

Nina's story poured out, "I couldn't stay in our home. I moved to another town to start over. I know the girls miss their friends and school." The women hugged. They discovered they only lived three hours apart and planned to visit.

The group watched the motorcades come from six directions. The memorial park was at the end of the Police Unity Tour. The next evening, they all attended the candlelight vigil. Kristi explained how local chapters of Badge of Courage support law enforcement and minister to them.

A month later Kristi felt the Lord wanted her to contact Nina, so she sent an encouraging email. Nina replied that she really needed it that day. It was her wedding anniversary and she was feeling very lonely. Nina said she knew God had sent Kristi and Rick into their lives to help them.

Talking with Kristi cheered Nina up. The mood changed and Kristi listened joyfully as Nina shared happy memories.

Bible Story Connection 3–4 minutes

Read 2 Samuel 9:1–12 and discover how King David took care
of his best friend's son after his best friend died in battle.

Chat Prompts

MORE TIME?

- *Do not be glad when the evil spirits obey you. Instead, be
glad that your names are written in heaven.* Luke 10:20

  It's sad that people die in what's called the "line of duty."
  Discuss safety and the danger law enforcement people
  face. Discuss the joy of knowing your name is in a
  memorial book, the Book of Life, and that one day all
  those who follow Jesus will be with him in Heaven.

- *You are my God. Please remember me and help me. Keep in
mind everything I've done for these people.* Nehemiah 5:19

  It's good to remember people we love who live
  in Heaven now. Have your parents share about
  family members who are in Heaven.

- *The names of those who do right are used in blessings. But
the names of those who do wrong will rot.* Proverbs 10:7

  Take some photos to keep as a memory of your family
  today. Let everyone share a good family memory.

Scrapbook/Prayer Journal Options

Make a memory page about Heaven.

- Draw a badge and write about laws and respecting law enforcement officers and following God's laws.

- Draw a rainbow. There's one in Heaven. Write about Heaven.

- Draw a picture of someone you love and write about a memory with that person.

Frontline Tips

- Our brains store happy memories in engram cells. Plan activities to create good memories and capture them with photos or writing about them.

- If a law enforcement family is struggling, encourage them to join the Fellowship of Christian Peace Officers or Badge of Hope. These organizations can be found online.

Prayer

Lord, help people in this nation respect law enforcement officers and the law of the land. Help keep safe the men and women who serve in law enforcement. In Jesus' name, amen.

Wrap-Up

Discuss ways to honor law enforcement officers.

Patience

Family Beatitude: Happy is the family who waits for a member returning home, for they will develop patience.

Focus: Waiting with patience

Weekly Bible Verse: *When Jesus returned, a crowd welcomed him. They were all expecting him.* Luke 8:40

Activity Options

☐ Fill days with cumulative activities. For example, draw a zoo and each day add a new animal. Or start a puzzle and add five pieces each day.

☐ Have children close their eyes and open them when they think a minute has passed. Who was the closest? Chat about how each minute brings us closer to being together again.

☐ If someone in your family has a friend away on a trip, make an activity book for them to do while they wait for the friend to come home.

The Waiting Tree 2 minutes

Whitney came home from preschool with a turkey made from a pine cone. She showed her mom and said, "Will Daddy be home for Thanksgiving?"

Her mother said, "Grandma and Papa are coming to celebrate. But, Daddy will not be home in time. We can be thankful every day. We can celebrate thanking God anytime."

Whitney jumped up and down and yelled, "Hoorah! I want to see Grandma and Papa. They've never come to Hawaii to visit us before. I miss them." Then she looked at her turkey and said, "I'm sad Daddy will be away. I'll still try to be thankful."

Every Thanksgiving, Whitney and her mom met with other Coast Guard families at the captain's house. This year Whitney's grandparents came, too. The house filled with friends whose dads also served on the ship. Since Whitney's grandfather was the only man there, the captain's wife asked him to carve the turkey. He laughed as children gathered around to watch.

A few weeks later, Whitney helped her mom put up a little Christmas tree. Her mom said, "This is the children's tree, so you can make and add an ornament every day. When it's full, Daddy will be here."

Whitney ran, grabbed her pine cone turkey and said, "I'll put this under the tree to remember to share it with Daddy.

When the tree seemed very full, her daddy came home, and she showed him the tree. He picked up the turkey and she said, "That was from Thanksgiving. You missed everything!"

Daddy hugged her and said, "I'm thankful to be here now. Let's thank God together."

Whitney laughed and said, "Mommy's right. We can be thankful any day."

Bible Story Connection 3–4 minutes

Read about Noah and his family waiting for
the flood to end in Genesis 8:6–14.

Chat Prompts

- *Love is patient. Love is kind. It does not want what belongs to others. It does not brag. It is not proud.* 1 Corinthians 13:4

  Chat about patience and waiting when it is hard.
  Discuss what to think about while waiting.

- *Anyone who is patient has great understanding. But anyone who gets angry quickly shows how foolish they are.* Proverbs 14:29

  How does patience help us be more
  understanding? Why is anger foolish?

- *We hope for what we don't have yet. So we are patient as we wait for it.* Romans 8:25

  Chat about how waiting develops patience. How does hope
  help us wait? What are you hoping and praying for now?

MORE TIME?

207

Scrapbook/Prayer Journal Options

Add a memory page about missing one another.

- Draw a clock and write about what helps you wait.

- Draw hearts and write about someone you love and miss.

- A camel can be a symbol for patience because it can go so long without water. Draw a camel and write about being patient.

Frontline Tips

- When a parent is away, have a daily time to chat and share good memories about that person. Pray for them.

- Hang up a Catch-Up Board to post photos of what the family member missed while away. Add notes and pictures. Let it become a talking wall to fill in the gaps when the family member returns. As a family, stand at the wall and share what each picture or note is about.

Prayer

Lord, keep our family members safe while apart and help us patiently wait to be reunited. In Jesus' name, amen.

Wrap-Up

Discuss patience and how to fill waiting times.

Faith Family

Family Beatitude: Happy is the family who knows they are children of God, for they belong to a larger family.

Focus: Connecting with others through faith

Weekly Bible Verse: *Those who are led by the Spirit of God are children of God.* Romans 8:14

Activity Options

☐ As a family, keep a file of addresses of friends. Encourage children to keep their own list of contacts, too.

☐ Make sure everyone in the family has a friend. Be hospitable to those friends. Rejoice if they are part of your faith family.

☐ Make paper airplanes and fly them toward one another. When you catch one, name a place you have lived or visited, a friend, or an activity you do with friends. Remember no matter where you move or travel, you can keep the friends you have and also make new ones.

Lasting Friends 2 minutes

"Dad, thanks for taking me to the father-daughter retreat this weekend. I had fun with you and I made some great friends."

At age twelve, Ashley lived in Washington D.C. where her dad was stationed in the Air Force. Her dad took her to a father-daughter retreat at White Sulphur Springs, an Officers' Christian Fellowship (OCF) retreat center for military families located in Pennsylvania.

Ashley stayed in touch with her new friends and spent time with them every summer at the retreat center. They roamed the woods, enjoyed programs, rode horses, swam, and canoed. More than that, they shared similar experiences as military kids and their faith in God. Each year they met others and made new friends! They became family and worked there together as teens. They even stayed close after Ashley moved to Korea by posting and chatting online.

One day, Ashley checked on her friends online. One of her friends, John, was now a soldier and had been injured in Afghanistan. The army flew John to Germany for surgery. Before he touched down, she heard that people in OCF in Germany, had traveled to be with John. The couples in Germany became surrogate parents as he recovered.

Ashley thought, "Now, that's family!" She felt so blessed to be part of such a caring organization.

Bible Story Connection 3–4 minutes

Read Ruth 1:1-18 about Naomi's family and how
things changed when they moved.

Chat Prompts

MORE TIME?

- *So when we can do good to everyone, let us do it. Let's try even harder to do good to the family of believers.* Galatians 6:10

  Who is in God's family? How should you treat those family members?

- *So you are no longer outsiders and strangers. You are citizens together with God's people. You are also members of God's family.* Ephesians 2:19

  Name some friends who are also believers in God's family.

- *Jesus, who makes people holy, and the people he makes holy belong to the same family. So Jesus is not ashamed to call them his brothers and sisters.* Hebrews 2:11

  Discuss God's family and how you can be close to those family members. What do you have in common?

Scrapbook/Prayer Journal Options

Add to your journal/scrapbook by writing about the family of God.

- Draw a tree and write about God's family tree.

- Draw smiling faces and name people in God's family.

- Add a cross and write about how people become part of God's family.

Frontline Tip

Make connections with other families who serve the way yours does. Encourage your children to make friend in these families. That gives them a friend who understands your unique life style.

Prayer

Thank you, Father, for giving us a larger family. Help us make good friends. In Jesus' name, amen.

Wrap-Up

Discuss your extended family of God.

Holiday Stress

Family Beatitude: Happy is the family that prays in emergencies, for they will be calm.

Focus: Remaining calm

Weekly Bible Verse: *Even though I walk through the darkest valley, I will not be afraid. You are with me. Your shepherd's rod and staff comfort me.* Psalm 23:4

Activity Options

☐ Practice ways to be calm like:

- ○ Taking deep breathes
- ○ Praying quietly
- ○ Counting slowly
- ○ Giving yourself a hug

☐ Take walks and do exercises to strengthen your heart.

☐ Keep a calming kit on hand for times the family feels stressed. Fill it with bubbles, Silly Putty, stress balls, and other items that help calm children.

☐ Keep supplies on hand to make thank you cards for people who help you when emergencies occur.

Cardiac Arrest 2 minutes

On Christmas Day, Tim and his partner, Mac, hopped in the ambulance to respond to a call about a cardiac arrest. It was the third 9-1-1 call that morning. Tim said, "Holidays are so hard. Christmas, it's usually elderly

with heart attacks and cardiac arrests. The Fourth of July is lots of men with burns. It's tough to see family gatherings face such trauma. Hopefully, any children will be calm and not screaming and crying."

They arrived and made their way to the patient. They noticed that several young children, ages six through ten, held hands and prayed quietly with the adults. Another adult was giving Cardiopulmonary resuscitation (CPR) to the grandfather.

The EMTs revived the man, got him on their stretcher and loaded the ambulance. Tim took a few minutes to help the children understand what happened. He explained, "Your grandfather's heart stopped beating and it's beating again now. The doctors will do their best to make him feel better and keep his heart beating."

The family expressed thanks and said in addition to praying for their grandfather, they would also pray for the EMTs and the ambulance driver.

The grandfather survived! The day after Christmas, the family visited the EMT base. They brought cookies and the children sang Christmas songs to express their thanks.

Bible Story Connection 3–4 minutes

Read Acts 28:1–5 about when a poisonous snake bit
Paul and he remained calm and unharmed.

Chat Prompts

MORE TIME?

- *The Levites calmed all the people down. They said, "Be quiet. This is a holy day. So don't be sad."* Nehemiah 8:11

  Talk about being calm when things go wrong, especially on a special day.

- *A person with a bad temper stirs up conflict. But a person who is patient calms things down.* Proverbs 15:18

  Discuss how words and actions can make us feel calm, nervous, angry, happy, or upset.

- *Don't worry about anything. No matter what happens, tell God about everything. Ask and pray, and give thanks to him.* Philippians 4:6

  Chat about how prayer helps us calm down and trust God, even in troubled times. Talk about how emergencies and problems help us be stronger.

Scrapbook/Prayer Journal Options

Add a holiday memory.

- Draw a stress ball and write ways to be calm.

- Draw a heart and write about heart health.

- Add a Christmas tree and write about how to make holidays into happy days.

Frontline Tips

- Families with emergency responders on call: plan some simple activities to do if a family member is called away. Resume the celebration when they return.

- Fill a box with activities like coloring books, puzzles, and Silly Putty to create a fun time if a family member must leave for a duty call.

Prayer

Lord, help us be calm and trust you every day, and especially when things don't go the way we hope. In Jesus' name, amen.

Wrap-Up

Discuss the best ways to remain calm.

Many Happy Returns

Family Beatitude: Happy is the family who values honesty, for they will develop integrity.

Focus: Developing character

Weekly Bible Verse: *The LORD has shown you what is good. He has told you what he requires of you. You must act with justice. You must love to show mercy. And you must be humble as you live in the sight of your God.* Micah 6:8

Activity Options

☐ Check out real and fake jewels. If you need to, go to stores that carry both types. Chat about how the real ones are much more valuable, but it can be difficult to tell them apart from the fake ones.

☐ Check out some optical illusions and chat about how they deceive us. How are lies deceptive? Try this one: With a marker, draw two arrows about an inch long, one on top of the other, both pointing in the same direction. Place the paper behind a clear glass and pour water to just above the lower arrow. It looks like the arrows are pointing in opposite directions. Fill the glass and you'll see the truth. Refraction causes the illusion.

☐ Write something but scramble the letters and words. See if others understand it. How are lies like scrambling the truth?

God Honors Faithfulness 2 minutes

Trev taught his oldest daughter Karlee how to count money. Soon after, they drove through a fast-food restaurant and the cashier handed back the change. Without counting it, Trev handed the money to Karlee and said, "Count this. There should be seven dollars."

She counted and said, "There are eight dollars."

Trev asked, "What's the right thing to do?"

Karlee replied, "Give back a dollar."

Trev smiled and said, "God will bless us for being honest and faithful."

A few months later, Trev took Karlee skiing. Once they got to the slopes, they realized Karlee had left her gloves at the cabin—five miles away! So they bought a new pair with nearly all the money Trev had with him. After skiing, they headed to the concession stand for water.

Exhausted from carrying the equipment, Trev asked a guy, "Can I set my equipment here?"

He replied, "Sure, Trevor."

Surprised to hear his name, Trev looked again and recognized a fellow firefighter from his department in Florida. He smiled, shook his hand, and said, "I'm so glad to see you! I'm sorry to ask, but could I borrow a few dollars for some drinks?"

His friend replied, "We have a cooler full of drinks. Take what you want and grab some snacks, too."

When they sat down, Trev said to Karlee, "God just blessed us for our faithfulness at that fast-food restaurant. The blessing circled back to us."

218

Bible Story Connection 3–4 minutes

Read 1 Samuel 17:26–50 and how David had learned to trust God's faithfulness when he took care of sheep. Read what happened to Ananias and Sapphira when they lied, in Acts 5:1–10.

Chat Prompts

MORE TIME?

- *You have done well, good and faithful slave! You have been faithful with a few things. I will put you in charge of many things. Come and share your master's happiness!* Matthew 25:21

    What happened to the faithful servant? How are we, as believers, like the slave? How is God like the master? How have you been blessed by being faithful?

- *The blessing of honest people builds up a city. But the words of sinners destroy it.* Proverbs 11:11

    How do honest people help a family and community be better?

- *He guards the path of those who are honest. He watches over the way of his faithful ones.* Proverbs 2:8

    What do you know God will do when you are honest and faithful? How have you seen God reward faithfulness?

219

Scrapbook/Prayer Journal Options

Create memory pages about faithfulness.

- Draw a dollar and write about honesty.

- Write or draw about a time God blessed your family.

- Draw or write about one of this week's verses.

Frontline Tips

- Discuss how people who serve others need to be honest and trustworthy. Consider how what they do puts them under greater scrutiny than people in other professions.

- Thank community workers for doing their jobs well and with honesty.

Prayer

Lord, help us be faithful and honest. In Jesus' name, amen.

Wrap-Up

Discuss ways to be faithful.

Kindness

Family Beatitude: Happy is the family who is kind, for they will bring joy to others.

Focus: Fostering kindness

Weekly Bible Verse *David asked, "Is anyone left from the royal house of Saul? If there is, I want to be kind to him because of Jonathan."* 2 Samuel 9:1

Activity Options

- ☐ Make a list of people you'd like to be kind to and think of something to do for each one.

- ☐ Periodically have a family circle of kindness. Sit in a circle as a family. Turn to the person next to you and give the person a compliment. That person then gives a compliment to the next person in the circle. Continue until the compliments go full circle. Go around the circle again and this time state one act of kindness to do for the next person. Then do that act sometime during the week.

- ☐ Use the grid on the next page to play Kindness Bingo and see how many squares each family member can check off in a week.

Be kind to animals	Clean the family car	Let a friend have the first turn	Read to a young child	Make a snack for someone
Pick up an item someone dropped	Help an elderly neighbor	Do someone else's chore	Help cook dinner	Collect food for a food pantry
Really listen to a friend	Pray for someone who is sick	Smile at everyone you see	Pick up litter to be kind to God's earth	Compliment someone
Thank a teacher or leader	Hug your mom or dad	Greet people at church	Give old toys to the poor	Say thanks to anyone who is kind
Thank the cook for your meals	Thank your pastor	Sit with someone who is alone	Hold the door for someone	Make treats for a neighbor

FAMILY DEVOTION · READ ALOUD ·

Respond with Kindness 2 minutes

The kids screamed and jumped up and down as the fire truck arrived. With the siren blasting, lights flashing, and Santa riding in front, the fire truck's arrival signaled the start of the annual Christmas party. Soon, the boys and girls smiled and laughed over the gifts they received.

The town had collected gifts for the families of the volunteer firefighters in appreciation for the many hours the firefighters spent keeping people and property safe. The lavish gifts surprised the children. One child shouted, "I got the special doll I wanted!"

Another yelled, "Yay! I got a skateboard!"

It's wonderful that people cared about the children and grandchildren of the volunteer firefighters. The party included a feast of delicious food, music, and entertainment. The children had done nothing directly to deserve the kindness.

When someone thanks a person for the service of their parents or other family members, it brings hope and pleasure to all members of the families.

Bible Story Connection 3–4 minutes

Long ago, Jonathan served the Israelites and befriended David. When David became king, after Jonathan's death in battle, he looked for a family member of Jonathan's to whom he could express his thanks. King David found Mephibosheth, Jonathan's son, and showered him with kindness. Read the story in 2 Samuel 9.

Chat Prompts

- *Mordecai sent letters to all the Jews in the 127 territories of the kingdom of Xerxes. The letters had messages of kindness and hope in them.* Esther 9:30

    Discuss how to show or express kindness. Share something kind someone said to you. Practice saying kind words.

MORE TIME?

- *The people of the island were unusually kind. It was raining and cold. So they built a fire and welcomed all of us.* Acts 28:2

    Talk about being kind when someone visits. Plan and prepare ways to welcome visitors kindly, including special snacks or a welcome packet.

- *Be kind and tender to one another. Forgive one another, just as God forgave you because of what Christ has done.* Ephesians 4:32

    Discuss how forgiving someone is an act of kindness. When have you forgiven someone? Ask God to help you be forgiving.

Scrapbook/Prayer Journal Options

Depict kindness with art.

- Draw Christmas symbols. Write acts of kindness done.

- Draw a circle with arrows to remember kindness is passed on and will circle back to you.

- Draw a table and place setting. Talk about being kind at meals.

Frontline Tip

Make an appreciation booklet or card to honor someone who helped your family during a hard time. Decorate it and write *High-Five to You for Being So Great.* List five reasons why you appreciate the person.

Scrapbook/Prayer Journal Options

Add a page on being thankful for family time around God's Word.

- Draw or trace hands and write ways to show gratitude on them.

- Draw a cross and around it write reasons to thank God.

- Draw a fire hat or other symbol of people who help us. Write words that express thanks for their sacrifices.

Prayer

Lord, thank you for being kind. Help us be kind to everyone we meet this week. In Jesus' name, amen.

Wrap-Up

Discuss the kindness activities you did and how they made you feel.